NO EASY DAY

THE FIRSTHAND ACCOUNT OF THE MISSION
THAT KILLED OSAMA BIN LADEN

NO EASY DAY

The Autobiography of a Navy SEAL

Mark Owen

with Kevin Maurer

DUTTON

DUTTON
Published by Penguin Group (USA) Inc.
375 Hudson Street, New York, New York 10014, U.S.A.
Penguin Group (Canada), 90 Eglinton Avenue East, Suite 700, Toronto, Ontario M4P
2Y3, Canada (a division of Pearson Penguin Canada Inc.); Penguin Books Ltd, 80 Strand,
London WC2R 0RL, England; Penguin Ireland, 25 St Stephen's Green, Dublin 2, Ireland
(a division of Penguin Books Ltd); Penguin Group (Australia), 250 Camberwell Road,
Camberwell, Victoria 3124, Australia (a division of Pearson Australia Group Pty Ltd);
Penguin Books India Pvt Ltd, 11 Community Centre, Panchsheel Park, New Delhi–110
017, India; Penguin Group (NZ), 67 Apollo Drive, Rosedale, Auckland 0632, New Zea-
land (a division of Pearson New Zealand Ltd); Penguin Books (South Africa) (Pty) Ltd, 24
Sturdee Avenue, Rosebank, Johannesburg 2196, South Africa

Penguin Books Ltd, Registered Offices: 80 Strand, London WC2R 0RL, England

Published by Dutton, a member of Penguin Group (USA) Inc.

First printing, September 2012
10 9 8 7 6 5 4 3 2 1

REGISTERED TRADEMARK—MARCA REGISTRADA

LIBRARY OF CONGRESS CATALOGING-IN-PUBLICATION DATA
has been applied for.

ISBN 978-0-525-95372-2

Printed in the United States of America
Set in Adobe Garamond Pro
Designed by Spring Hoteling
Photographs are from the author's collection.
Maps by Travis Rightmeyer

The publisher acknowledges that the name Mark Owen is a pseudonym.

ALWAYS LEARNING   PEARSON

The only easy day was yesterday.

—Navy SEAL Philosophy

Long live the Brotherhood.

CONTENTS

CONTENTS

AUTHOR'S NOTE

When I was in junior high school in Alaska, we were assigned a book report. We had to pick a book we liked. Moving down the row of books, I stumbled upon *Men in Green Faces* by former SEAL Gene Wentz. The novel chronicled missions in Vietnam's Mekong Delta. Full of ambushes and firefights, it centered on the hunt for a rogue North Vietnamese colonel.

From page one, I knew I wanted to be a SEAL. The more I read, the more I wanted to see if I could measure up.

In the surf of the Pacific Ocean during training, I found other men just like me: men who feared failure and were driven to be the best. I was privileged to serve with and be inspired by these men every day. Working alongside them made me a better person.

After thirteen consecutive combat deployments, my war is over. This book is closure for that part of my life. Before leaving, I wanted to try and explain what it was that motivated us through the brutal SEAL training course and through a decade of constant deployments.

We are not superheroes, but we all share a common bond in serving something greater than ourselves. It is a brotherhood that ties us together, and that bond is what allows us to willingly walk into harm's way together.

This is the story of a group of extraordinary men who I was lucky enough to serve alongside as a SEAL from 1998 to 2012. I've changed the names of all the characters, including myself, to protect our identities, and this book does not include details of any ongoing missions.

I've also taken great pains to protect the tactics, techniques, and procedures used by the teams as they wage a daily battle against terrorists and insurgents around the world. If you are looking for secrets, this is not your book.

Although I am writing this book in an effort to accurately describe real-world events as they occurred, it is important to me that no classified information is released. With the assistance of my publisher, I hired a former Special Operations attorney to review the manuscript to ensure that it was free from mention of forbidden topics and that it cannot be used by sophisticated enemies as a source of sensitive information to compromise or harm the United States. I am confident that the team that has worked with me on this book has both maintained and promoted the security interests of the United States.

When I refer to other military or government organizations, activities, or agencies, I do so in the interest of continuity and normally only if another publication or official unclassified government document has already mentioned that organization's participation in the mission I'm describing.

I sometimes refer to certain publicly recognized senior military leaders by their true names, only when it is clear that there are no operational security issues involved. In all other cases, I have intentionally depersonalized the stories to maintain the anonymity of the individuals involved. I do not describe any technologies that would compromise the security of the United States.

All of the material contained within this book is derived from unclassified publications and sources; nothing written here is intended to confirm or deny, officially or unofficially, any events described or the activities of any individual, government, or agency. In an effort to protect the nature of specific operations, I sometimes generalize dates, times, and order of events. None of these "work-arounds" affect the accuracy of my recollections or my description of how events unfolded. The operations discussed in this book have been written about in numerous other civilian and government publications and are available in open sources to the general public. These confirming open-source citations are printed in the Confirming Sources list at the end of this book.

The events depicted in *No Easy Day* are based on my own memory. Conversations have been reconstructed from my recollections. War is chaotic, but I have done my best to ensure the stories in this book are accurate. If there are inaccuracies in it, the responsibility is mine. This book presents my views and does not represent the views of the United States Navy, the U.S. Department of Defense, or anyone else.

In spite of the deliberate measures I have undertaken to protect the national security of the United States and the operational security of the men and women who continue to fight around the world, I believe *No Easy Day* to be an accurate portrayal of the events it describes and an honest portrayal of life in the SEAL teams and the brotherhood that exists among us. While written in the first person, my experiences are universal, and I'm no better or worse than any man I've served with. It was a long, hard decision to write this book, and some in the community will look down on me for doing so.

However, it is time to set the record straight about one of the most important missions in U.S. military history. Lost in the media coverage of the Bin Laden raid is why and how the mission was successful. This book will finally give credit to those who earned it. The mission was a team effort, from the intelligence analysts who found Osama bin Laden to the helicopter pilots who flew us to Abbottabad to the men who assaulted the compound. No one man or woman was more important than another.

No Easy Day is the story of "the guys," the human toll we pay, and the sacrifices we make to do this dirty job. This book is about a brotherhood that existed long before I joined and will be around long after I am gone.

My hope is one day a young man in junior high school will read it and become a SEAL, or at least live a life bigger than him. If that happens, the book is a success.

Mark Owen
June 22, 2012,
Virginia Beach, Virginia

NO EASY DAY

Chalk One

At one minute out, the Black Hawk crew chief slid the door open.

I could just make him out—his night vision goggles covering his eyes—holding up one finger. I glanced around and saw my SEAL teammates calmly passing the sign throughout the helicopter.

The roar of the engine filled the cabin, and it was now impossible to hear anything other than the Black Hawk's rotors beating the air. The wind buffeted me as I leaned out, scanning the ground below, hoping to steal a glance of the city of Abbottabad.

An hour and a half before, we'd boarded our two MH-60

Black Hawks and lifted off into a moonless night. It was only a short flight from our base in Jalalabad, Afghanistan, to the border with Pakistan, and from there another hour to the target we had been studying on satellite images for weeks.

The cabin was pitch-black except for the lights from the cockpit. I had been wedged against the left door with no room to stretch out. We'd stripped the helicopter of its seats to save on weight, so we either sat on the floor or on small camp chairs purchased at a local sporting goods store before we left.

Now perched on the edge of the cabin, I stretched my legs out the door trying to get the blood flowing. My legs were numb and cramped. Crowded into the cabin around me and in the second helicopter were twenty-three of my teammates from the Naval Special Warfare Development Group, or DEVGRU. I had operated with these men dozens of times before. Some I had known ten years or more. I trusted each one completely.

Five minutes ago, the whole cabin had come alive. We pulled on our helmets and checked our radios and then made one final check of our weapons. I was wearing sixty pounds of gear, each gram meticulously chosen for a specific purpose, my load refined and calibrated over a dozen years and hundreds of similar missions.

This team had been handpicked, assembled of the most experienced men in our squadron. Over the last forty-eight hours, as go day loomed and then was postponed and then loomed again, we had each checked and rechecked our equipment so we were more than ready for this night.

This was a mission I'd dreamt about since I watched the September 11, 2001, attacks on a TV in my barracks room in Okinawa. I was just back from training and got into my room in time to see the second plane crash into the World Trade Center. I couldn't turn away as the fireball shot out of the opposite side of the building and smoke billowed out of the tower.

Like millions of Americans back home, I stood there watching in disbelief with a hopeless feeling in the pit of my stomach. I stayed transfixed to the screen for the rest of the day as my mind tried to make sense of what I'd just witnessed. One plane crash could be an accident. The unfolding news coverage confirmed what I had known the moment the second plane entered the TV shot. A second plane was an attack, no doubt. No way that happened by accident.

On September 11, 2001, I was on my first deployment as a SEAL, and as Osama bin Laden's name was mentioned I figured my unit would get the call to go to Afghanistan the next day. For the previous year and a half, we'd been training to deploy. We'd trained in Thailand, the Philippines, East Timor, and Australia over the last few months. As I watched the attacks, I longed to be out of Okinawa and in the mountains of Afghanistan, chasing al Qaeda fighters and serving up a little payback.

We never got the call.

I was frustrated. I hadn't trained so hard and for so long to become a SEAL only to watch the war on TV. Of course, I wasn't about to let my family and friends in on my frustration.

They were writing asking me if I was going to Afghanistan. To them, I was a SEAL and it was only logical that we would be immediately deployed to Afghanistan.

I remember that I sent an e-mail to my girlfriend at the time trying to make light of a bad situation. We were talking about the end of this deployment and making plans for my time at home before the next deployment.

"I've got about a month left," I wrote. "I'll be home soon, unless I have to kill Bin Laden first." It was the kind of joke you heard a lot back then.

Now, as the Black Hawks flew toward our target, I thought back over the last ten years. Ever since the attacks, everyone in my line of work had dreamt of being involved in a mission like this. The al Qaeda leader personified everything we were fighting against. He'd inspired men to fly planes into buildings filled with innocent civilians. That kind of fanaticism is scary, and as I watched the towers crumble and saw reports of attacks in Washington, D.C., and Pennsylvania, I knew we were at war, and not a war of our choosing. A lot of brave men had sacrificed for years to fight the war, never knowing if we would get a chance to be involved in a mission like the one about to begin.

A decade after that event and with eight years of chasing and killing al Qaeda's leaders, we were minutes away from fast-roping into Bin Laden's compound.

Grabbing the rope attached to the Black Hawk's fuselage, I could feel the blood finally returning to my toes. The sniper next to me slid into place with one leg hanging outside and one leg inside the helicopter so that there was more room in the already-tight doorway. The barrel of his weapon was scanning for targets in the compound. His job was to cover the south side of the compound as the assault team fast-roped into the courtyard and split up to our assignments.

Just over a day ago, none of us had believed Washington would approve the mission. But after weeks of waiting, we were now less than a minute from the compound. The intelligence said our target would be there; I figured he was, but nothing would surprise me. We'd thought we were close a couple times before.

I had spent a week in 2007 chasing rumors of Bin Laden. We had received reports that he was coming back into Afghanistan from Pakistan for a final stand. A source said he'd seen a man in "flowing white robes" in the mountains. After weeks of prep, it was ultimately a wild-goose chase. This time felt different. Before we left, the CIA analyst who was the main force behind tracking the target to Abbottabad said she was one hundred percent certain he was there. I hoped she was right, but my experience told me to reserve judgment until the mission was over.

It didn't matter now. We were seconds away from the house and whoever was living in there was about to have a bad night.

We had completed similar assaults countless times before. For the last ten years, I had deployed to Iraq, Afghanistan, and to the Horn of Africa. We had been part of the mission to rescue Richard Phillips, the captain of the container ship

Maersk Alabama, from three Somali pirates in 2009, and I had operated in Pakistan before. Tactically, tonight was no different from a hundred other operations; historically, I hoped it was going to be very different.

As soon as I gripped the rope, a calm came over me. Everyone on the mission had heard that one-minute call a thousand times before and at this point it was no different than any other operation. From the door of the helicopter, I started to make out landmarks I recognized from studying satellite images of the area during our weeks of training. I wasn't clipped into the helicopter with a safety line, so my teammate Walt had a hand on a nylon loop on the back of my body armor. Everybody was crowding toward the door right behind me ready to follow me down. On the right side, my teammates had a good visual of the trail helicopter with Chalk Two heading to its landing zone.

As soon as we cleared the southeastern wall, our helicopter flared out and started to hover near our predetermined insert point. Looking down thirty feet into the compound, I could see laundry whipping on a clothesline. Rugs hung out to dry were battered by dust and dirt from the rotors. Trash swirled around the yard, and in a nearby animal pen, goats and cows thrashed around, startled by the helicopter.

Focused on the ground, I could see we were still over the guesthouse. As the helicopter rocked, I could tell the pilot was having some trouble getting the aircraft into position. We veered between the roof of the guesthouse and the wall of the compound. Glancing over at the crew chief, I could see he had his radio microphone pressed against his mouth, passing directions to the pilot.

The helicopter was bucking as it tried to find enough air to set a stable hover and hold station. The wobbling wasn't violent, but I could tell it wasn't planned. The pilot was fighting the controls trying to correct it. Something wasn't right. The pilots had done this kind of mission so many times that for them putting a helicopter over a target was like parking a car.

Staring into the compound, I considered throwing the rope just so we could get out of the unstable bird. I knew it was a risk, but getting on the ground was imperative. There wasn't anything I could do stuck in the door of the helicopter. All I needed was a clear spot to throw the rope.

But the clear spot never came.

"We're going around. We're going around," I heard over the radio. That meant the original plan to fast-rope into the compound was now off. We were going to circle around to the south, land, and assault from outside the wall. It would add precious time to the assault and allow anyone inside the compound more time to arm themselves.

My heart sank.

Up until I heard the go-around call, everything was going as planned. We had evaded the Pakistani radar and anti-aircraft missiles on the way in and arrived undetected. Now, the insert was already going to shit. We had rehearsed this contingency, but it was plan B. If our target was really inside, surprise was the key and it was quickly slipping away.

As the helicopter attempted to climb out of its unstable

hover, it took a violent right turn, spinning ninety degrees. I could feel the tail kick to the left. It caught me by surprise and I immediately struggled to find a handhold inside the cabin to keep from sliding out the door.

I could feel my butt coming off the floor, and for a second I could feel a panic rising in my chest. I let go of the rope and started to lean back into the cabin, but my teammates were all crowded in the door. There was little room for me to scoot back. I could feel Walt's grip tighten on my body armor as the helicopter started to drop. Walt's other hand held the sniper's gear. I leaned back as far as I could. Walt was practically lying on top of me to keep me inside.

"Holy fuck, we're going in," I thought.

The violent turn put my door in the front as the helicopter started to slide sideways. I could see the wall of the courtyard coming up at us. Overhead, the engines, which had been humming, now seemed to scream as they tried to beat the air into submission to stay aloft.

The tail rotor had barely missed hitting the guesthouse as the helicopter slid to the left. We had joked before the mission that our helicopter had the lowest chance of crashing because so many of us had already survived previous helicopter crashes. We'd been sure if a helicopter was going to crash it would be the one carrying Chalk Two.

Thousands of man-hours, maybe even millions, had been spent leading the United States to this moment, and the mission was about to go way off track before we even had a chance to get our feet on the ground.

I tried to kick my legs up and wiggle deeper into the cabin.

If the helicopter hit on its side, it might roll, trapping my legs under the fuselage. Leaning back as far as I could, I pulled my legs into my chest. Next to me, the sniper tried to clear his legs from the door, but it was too crowded. There was nothing we could do but hope the helicopter didn't roll and chop off his exposed leg.

Everything slowed down. I tried to push the thoughts of being crushed out of my mind. With every second, the ground got closer and closer. I felt my whole body tense up, ready for the inevitable impact.

CHAPTER I

Green Team

I could feel the sweat dripping down my back, soaking my shirt, as I slowly moved down the corridor of the kill house at our training site in Mississippi.

It was 2004, seven years before I would ride a Black Hawk into Abbottabad, Pakistan, on one of the most historic special operations raids in history. I was in the selection and training course for SEAL Team Six, sometimes called by its full name: United States Naval Special Warfare Development Group, abbreviated DEVGRU. The nine-month selection course was known as Green Team, and it was the one thing that stood between me and the other candidates moving up to the elite DEVGRU.

My heart was beating fast, and I had to blink the perspiration out of my eyes as I followed my teammate to the door. My breathing was labored and ragged as I tried to force any extraneous thoughts from my head. I was nervous and edgy, and that was how mistakes were made. I needed to focus, but no matter what was in the room we were about to enter, it paled compared to the cadre of instructors watching on the catwalk.

All of the instructors were senior combat veterans from DEVGRU. Handpicked to train new operators, they held my future in their hands.

"Just get to lunch," I muttered to myself.

It was the only way I could control my anxiety. In 1998, I'd made it through Basic Underwater Demolition/SEAL, or BUD/S, by focusing on just making it to the next meal. It didn't matter if I couldn't feel my arms as we hoisted logs over our heads or if the cold surf soaked me to the core. It wasn't going to last forever. There is a saying: "How do you eat an elephant?" The answer is simple: "One bite at a time." Only my bites were separated by meals: Make it to breakfast, train hard until lunch, and focus until dinner. Repeat.

In 2004, I was already a SEAL, but making it to DEVGRU would be the pinnacle of my career. As the Navy's counter-terrorism unit, DEVGRU did hostage rescue missions, tracked war criminals, and, since the attacks on September 11, hunted and killed al Qaeda fighters in Afghanistan and Iraq.

But nothing about making it through Green Team was easy. It was no longer good enough for me to be a SEAL. During Green Team, just passing was failing and second place was the first loser. The point was not to meet the minimums, but crush them. Success in Green Team was about managing stress and performing at your peak level—all the time.

Before each training day, we completed a punishing phys-ical training or PT workout of long runs, push-ups, pull-ups, and anything else the sadistic instructors could cook up. We pushed cars, and on multiple occasions we pushed buses. When we got to the kill house, a purpose-built ballistically safe building made up of hallways and rooms used to practice close-quarters battle, or CQB, our muscles were already tired and sore. The point of doing the PT was to make us physically tired to simulate the stress of a real mission before they tested us in a demanding tactical environment.

I didn't have time to steal a glimpse at the instructors as we moved down the hall. This was the first day of training, and everybody's nerves were running high. We had started CQB training after completing a full month's worth of high-altitude parachute training in Arizona. The pressure to per-form had been evident there too, but once we got to Mississippi it was ratcheted up.

I shook the nagging aches and pains from my mind and concentrated on the door in front of me. It was made of thin plywood with no doorknob. The door was battered and bro-ken from teams that went before us, and my teammate easily pushed it open with his gloved hand. We paused for a second at the threshold, scanning for targets before we entered.

The room was square, with rough walls made of old railroad ties to absorb the live rounds. I could hear my teammate enter behind me as I swept my rifle in an arc searching for a target.

Nothing. The room was empty.

"Moving," my teammate called as he stepped into the room to clear around a corner.

Instinctually, I slid into position to cover him.

As soon as I started to move, I could hear murmuring above me in the rafters. We couldn't stop, but I knew one of us had just made a mistake. For a second, my stress level spiked, but I quickly pushed it out of my mind. There was no time to worry about mistakes. There were more rooms to clear. I couldn't worry about the mistakes I made in the first room.

Back in the hall, we entered the next room. I spotted two targets as I entered. To the right, I saw the silhouette of a crook holding a small revolver. He was wearing a sweatshirt and looked like a 1970s thug from the movies. To the left, there was a silhouette of a woman holding a purse.

I snapped a shot off at the crook seconds after stepping into the room. The round hit center mass. I moved toward it, shooting a few more rounds.

"Clear," I said, lowering my muzzle.

"Clear," my teammate answered.

"Safe 'em and let 'em hang," one of the instructors said from above.

No less than six instructors were looking down at us from a catwalk that spidered out over the kill house. They could walk safely along the walkways watching as we cleared the different rooms, judging our performance and watching for any tiny mistakes.

I put my rifle on safe and let it hang against me by its sling. I wiped beads of sweat out of my eyes with my sleeve. My heart was still pounding, even though we were finished. The training scenarios were pretty straightforward. We all knew how to clear rooms. It was the process of clearing a room perfectly under the simulated stress of combat that would set us apart.

There was no margin of error, and at that moment I wasn't sure exactly what we had done wrong.

"Where was your move call?" Tom, one of the instructors, said to me from the catwalk.

I didn't answer. I just nodded. I was embarrassed and disappointed. I'd forgotten to tell my teammate to move in the first room, which was a safety violation.

Tom was one of the best instructors in the course. I could always pick him out because he had a huge head. It was massive, like it housed a giant brain. It was his one distinct physical trait; otherwise you'd miss him because he was mellow and never seemed to get upset. We all respected him because he was both firm and fair. When you made a mistake in front of Tom, it felt like you let him down. His disappointment with me was plastered across his face.

No screaming.

No yelling.

Just the look.

From above, I saw him shoot me the *"Dude, really? Did you just do that?"* look.

I wanted to speak or at least try and explain, but I knew they didn't want to hear it. If they said you were wrong, you were wrong. Standing below them in the empty room, there was no arguing or explaining.

"OK, check," I said, defenseless and furious with myself for making such a basic error.

"We need better than that," Tom said. "Beat it. Do your ladder climb."

Snatching up my rifle, I jogged out of the kill house and sprinted to a rope ladder hanging on a tree about three hundred yards away. Climbing up the ladder, rung by rung, I felt heavier. It wasn't my sweat-soaked shirt or the sixty pounds of body armor and gear strapped to my chest.

It was my fear of failure. I've never failed anything in my SEAL career.

When I got to San Diego six years earlier for BUD/S, I never doubted I'd make it. A lot of my fellow BUD/S candidates who arrived with me either got cut or quit. Some of them couldn't keep up with the brutal beach runs, or they panicked underwater during SCUBA training.

Like a lot of other BUD/S candidates, I knew I wanted to become a SEAL when I was thirteen. I read every book I could find about the SEALs, followed the news during Desert Storm for any mention of them, and daydreamed about ambushes and coming up over the beach on a combat mission. I wanted to do all of the things I'd read in the books while growing up.

After completing my degree at a small college in California, I went to BUD/S and earned my SEAL trident in 1998. After a six-month deployment throughout the Pacific Rim, and a combat deployment to Iraq in 2003–2004, I was ready for something new. I'd learned about DEVGRU during my first two deployments. DEVGRU was a collection of the best the SEAL community had to offer, and I knew I would never be able to live with myself if I didn't try.

The Navy's counter-terrorism unit was born in the aftermath of Operation Eagle Claw, the failed 1980 mission ordered by President Jimmy Carter to rescue fifty-two Americans held captive at the U.S. Embassy in Tehran, Iran.

After the mission, the Navy identified a need for a force capable of successfully executing those kind of specialized missions and tapped Richard Marcinko to develop a maritime counter-terrorism unit called SEAL Team Six. The team practiced hostage rescue as well as infiltrating enemy countries, ships, naval bases, and oil rigs. Over time, missions branched out to counter-proliferation of weapons of mass destruction.

At the time Marcinko established the command, there were only two SEAL teams, so "six" was chosen to make the Soviets think the Navy had more teams. In 1987, SEAL Team Six became DEVGRU.

The unit started with seventy-five operators, handpicked by Marcinko. Now, all of the members of the unit are handpicked from other SEAL teams and Explosive Ordnance Disposal units. The unit has grown significantly and filled out with numerous teams of operators as well as support staff, but the concept remains the same.

The unit is part of the Joint Special Operations Command, called JSOC. DEVGRU works closely with other National Missions Force teams like the Army's Delta Force.

One of DEVGRU's first missions was in 1983 during Operation Urgent Fury. Members of the unit rescued Grenada's governor-general, Paul Scoon, during the U.S.–led invasion of the small Caribbean nation after a Communist takeover. Scoon was facing execution.

Six years later in 1989, DEVGRU joined with Delta Force to capture Manuel Noriega during the invasion of Panama.

DEVGRU operators were part of the U.S.–led mission to capture Somali warlord Mohamed Farrah Aidid in October 1993, which turned into the Battle of Mogadishu. The fight was chronicled in Mark Bowden's book *Black Hawk Down*.

In 1998, DEVGRU operators tracked Bosnian war criminals, including Radislav Krstić, the Bosnian general who was later indicted for his role in the Srebrenica massacre of 1995.

Since September 11, 2001, DEVGRU operators had been on a steady cycle of deployments to Iraq and Afghanistan, targeting al Qaeda and Taliban commanders. The command got the immediate call to insert into Afghanistan after September 11, 2001, and operators in the command were responsible for some of the high-profile missions like the Jessica Lynch rescue in Iraq in 2003. It was missions like these and the fact that they are the first to get the call that motivated me.

Before you can screen for Green Team, you need to be a SEAL, and most candidates typically have two deployments. The deployments usually mean the candidate has the necessary skill level and experience, which was needed to complete the selection course.

As I climbed the rungs on the ladder in the Mississippi heat, I couldn't help but think about how I'd almost failed the three-day screening process before even starting Green Team.

The dates for the screening fell during my unit's land warfare training. I was at Camp Pendleton, California, hiding under a tree, watching Marines build a base camp. It was 2003 and we were a week into our reconnaissance training block when I got orders to report back to San Diego to start the three-day screening process. If I was lucky enough to get selected, I would begin the nine-month Green Team training course. If I was lucky enough to pass, I would join the ranks of DEVGRU.

I was the only one in my platoon going. A buddy in a sister platoon was also screening. As we drove down together, we both were washing the green paint off our faces. Still dressed in our camouflage uniforms, we smelled of body odor and bug spray after spending days in the field. My stomach hurt from eating nothing but Meals, Ready-To-Eat, and I tried to hydrate, sucking down water as we drove. I was not in the best physical shape, and I knew the first part of the screening was a fitness test.

The next morning, we were out at the beach. The sun was just peeking over the horizon as I finished the four-mile timed run. After a short break, I joined about two dozen other candidates in a line on a concrete pad. A breeze blew off the Pacific, and there was a little chill in the air from the night before. At any other time, it would have been a pretty morning on the beach. I was already tired from the run, and we still had push-ups, sit-ups, and pull-ups before the swim.

I easily passed the push-up test, despite the instructors' nitpicking each rep. Every exercise had to be perfect, or it didn't count. Rolling onto my back, I prepared for the sit-up test.

I was really tired as I knocked out the first sit-ups.

Being out in the field hadn't helped my stamina. I got into a good rhythm at first, but it was broken when the instructor stopped next to me and started repeating some of the numbers of my reps.

"Ten, ten, ten," he said. "Ten, eleven, twelve, twelve."

My technique wasn't textbook. He was repeating the numbers that weren't perfect. Every time he repeated a number, I was more ashamed. I was getting tired but I wasn't getting any closer to meeting the test standard.

"One minute."

I was way behind as the call came and was quickly running out of time. If I failed the sit-ups, I was done. Doubt started to creep into my mind. I started to come up with bullshit excuses like I was ill-prepared because I had been training with my unit, rather than preparing for this test.

"Thirty seconds."

With half a minute to go I was ten short of the minimum number. Next to me, another guy had already passed that number and he was knocking out even more as fast as he could go. My mind was spinning and I couldn't believe I was failing. Forcing the poisonous thoughts from my mind, I focused on technique. Soon, I was making up ground.

"Ten seconds."

I was close. My stomach ached. My breath came in gasps. My fatigue was replaced with fear. I was in shock. I couldn't fail. There was no way I could go back to my platoon knowing I couldn't even pass the physical fitness test.

"Five, four, three . . ."

As the instructors called time, I finished my last sit-up. I squeaked by, passing the minimum by two measly sit-ups. I was spent, but I still had to do the pull-ups. Walking to the bar, the near-failure scared some adrenaline into me and I was able to pass the pull-ups without issue.

The final event was a swim in San Diego Bay. The water was calm. We had wetsuits on, so I couldn't feel the chill of the water. I started strong. One of the guys screening had been a Naval Academy swimmer and was well ahead of me, but I was in second place. I kept pulling, but it felt like I was going slow. It felt like swimming on a treadmill.

When I got to the finish line, the instructors told me I'd failed. It turned out everyone except for the academy swimmer failed. That caught the attention of the instructors and they checked the tide schedule. After a quick review of the currents, word came down that we had been swimming against the tide.

"We're going to do the whole test again tomorrow," they told us, to my relief.

Part of the challenge was that you're tired by the time you get to each exercise. So we couldn't just repeat the swim. I knew I would have to do the sit-ups again and in the back of my mind, I knew I wasn't going to get my abs in shape in one night.

It was a mental thing.

I went in there ready to kick ass the next day, and I willed my way to a passing score. I knew my scores weren't great, and I was concerned about how they'd be received during the oral board the next day. Just because I passed the minimum scores didn't mean anything in the big scheme of things. This was a selection course for the best of the best, and I was not showing the instructors that I was prepared.

I arrived early for my interview in my dress blue uniform with all of my ribbons and awards. I'd gotten a haircut the day before and made sure my shave was close. I looked like a diagram out of a uniform textbook. It was one of the rare times I knew a haircut, shined shoes, and a pressed uniform really mattered for a SEAL. At least it gave the instructors one less thing to pick on during the board.

Inside the conference room was a long table at the far end. Seated at the table were a half dozen master chiefs, a psychologist who had tested us the second day of screening, and a career counselor. A single chair sat in front of the board. I walked into the room and took a seat.

For the next forty-five minutes, they took turns lobbing questions at me. I'd never been under fire like this. I didn't know that before I arrived, the board had already talked to my platoon chief and commander at SEAL Team Five. They had an idea of who I was, but this was the only time they'd get a chance to size me up in person.

To this day, I can't remember who sat on my oral board. To me, they were just high-ranking operators who held my future in their hands. It was up to me to convince them to select me.

But my poor physical fitness score wasn't helping my case.

"Do you know who you are screening for?" one of the chiefs said. "Do you know what you're trying out to do? This is the entry-level test. You're getting ready for the big leagues here and this is what you show?"

I didn't hesitate. I knew they'd hit me on this and I only had one play.

"I take full responsibility," I said. "I am embarrassed to sit here and show you that PT score. All I can tell you is if I show up, if I am selected, those scores are never going to happen again. I am not going to give you any excuses. That is on me. It is on nobody but myself."

I searched their faces to see if they believed me. There was no indication if they did or not. All I got were blank stares. The barrage of questions continued, designed to keep me off balance. They wanted to see if I could keep my composure. If

I can't sit in a chair and answer questions, then what am I going to do under fire? If they wanted to make me uncomfortable, they succeeded, but mostly I was embarrassed. These were people who I looked up to and aspired to be like and here I was, a young SEAL who had barely passed his sit-up test.

At the end of the board, they dismissed me.

"We'll let you know within the next six months if you have been selected."

As I left the room I figured I had a fifty-fifty chance of making it.

Back at Camp Pendleton, I smeared fresh green paint on my face and snuck back into the field to join my teammates for the last few days of the training mission.

"How did it go?" my chief asked when I linked up with the team.

"I don't know," I said.

I wasn't telling anyone about the fitness test. I knew there was a real chance I had failed.

I was in the middle of my SEAL Team Five deployment to Iraq when I finally got the news. My platoon chief called me into our operations center.

"You screened positive," he said. "You'll be getting orders to Green Team when we get back."

I was shocked because in my mind I had been preparing myself for the worst. I had it in my head I would have to re-screen. Now that I had been selected, I was committed to not making the same mistakes. I knew I would show up at Green Team prepared.

CHAPTER 2

Top Five/Bottom Five

My lungs burned and my legs ached as I ran back from the ladder in the humid Mississippi summer. The pain was less physical and more about pride. I was screwing up. The pressure I was putting on myself was worse than anything I'd hear from the instructors. The mistake I'd made in the kill house was a result of losing focus, and I knew that was unacceptable. I knew I wouldn't be in the course much longer if I couldn't block out the pressure and focus on the tasks at hand. Candidates could get cut from the course on any given day.

I ran back and stood outside the house. I could hear the crack of rifle fire inside as other teams cleared rooms. We had a few minutes to catch our breath before going back in for yet another iteration.

Tom had climbed down from the catwalk and was outside when I got back. He pulled me aside.

"Hey, brother," he said. "It was exactly the right move in there. You covered your buddy, but there was no 'moving' call."

"Check," I said.

"I know back in your old command you guys did things your way and maybe you didn't need the call there," Tom said. "But here, we want textbook CQB and we want the verbage we asked for. If you are lucky to complete this training and go to an assault squadron on the second deck, trust me, you won't be doing basic CQB. But here, under pressure, you need to prove to us that you can do even the most basic CQB. We have a standard, and you can't move without a moving call."

The "second deck" was where all of the assault squadrons worked at the command back in Virginia Beach. During our first days in Green Team, we were told we were not allowed to go up to the second floor of the building. It was off-limits until graduation.

So, getting to the second deck was the goal. It was the prize.

I nodded and slid a new magazine into my rifle.

That night, I grabbed a cold beer and spread my cleaning kit out on the table. I took a long pull and savored the fact I survived, another bite out of the proverbial elephant. I was one step closer to the second deck.

During our CQB block of training, we lived in two large

houses located near the shooting ranges and kill house. They were basically massive barracks beat to hell after hundreds of SEAL and Special Forces training rotations. The rooms were filled with bunk beds, but I spent most of my time downstairs in the lounge area. There was a pool table and a 1980s big screen TV usually tuned to a sporting event. It was more background noise as guys cleaned their weapons or shot pool and tried to unwind.

The SEAL community is small. We all know each other or have at least heard of one another. From the day you step onto the beach to start BUD/S, you are building a reputation. Everybody talks about reputation from day one.

"Saw you on the ladder today," Charlie said to me as he racked up the balls for another game of pool. "What did you fuck up?"

Charlie was big in both stature and wit. He was a huge man with hands the size of shovels and giant shoulders. Standing about six foot four inches tall, he weighed in at two hundred and thirty pounds. His mouth was as big as his body. He kept up a steady stream of smack talk, day and night.

We called him "the Bully."

A former deck seaman, Charlie grew up in the Midwest and joined the Navy after graduation. He spent about a year chipping paint and brawling with his crewmates in the fleet before going to BUD/S. The way Charlie told it, being out in the fleet was like being in a gang. He told stories about fights on the ship and in port or on cruise. He hated being on the ships and wanted nothing more than to become a SEAL.

Charlie was one of the top candidates in the class. He was consistently smart and aggressive, and it didn't hurt that his last job before Green Team was as a CQB instructor for the East Coast SEAL Teams. The kill houses came naturally to him. And he was a crack shot to boot.

"No move call," I said.

"Keep it up and you'll be back in San Diego working on that tan," he said. "At least you'll be ready for next year's calendar."

SEALs are based in two places—San Diego, California, and Virginia Beach, Virginia. A healthy rivalry existed between the two groups, based mostly on geography and demographics. The difference between the teams is minimal. Teams on both coasts did the same missions and had the same skill set. But West Coast SEALs have the reputation of being laid-back surfers and the East Coast guys are thought of as Carhartt-wearing rednecks.

I was a West Coast SEAL, so hanging with Charlie meant a steady diet of digs, especially about the calendar.

"Right, Mr. May?" Charlie said, snickering.

I didn't appear in it, but some of the teammates put out a calendar a few years back for charity. The pictures were cringe-worthy shots of guys without shirts on the beach or near the gray-hulled ships in San Diego. The move may have helped feed the poor or fight cancer, but it brought on years of mocking from the East Coast teams.

"No one wants to make a calendar of pasty white East Coast guys," I said. "I am sorry if we have our shirts off enjoying the sunny San Diego weather."

It was a battle that would never end.

"We'll settle this on the range tomorrow," I said.

My fallback was always shooting. I didn't have the wit to go up against Charlie or the other smooth talkers in Green Team. It was widely known that my jokes were always weak. It was better to beat a quick retreat and then do my best to outshoot those guys the next day. I was an above-average shot, since I'd pretty much grown up with a gun in my hand during my childhood in Alaska.

My parents never let me play with toy guns because by the time I was finished with elementary school I was carrying a .22 rifle. From an early age, I knew the responsibility of handling a firearm. For our family, a gun was a tool.

"You need to respect the gun and respect what it can do," my father told me.

He taught me how to shoot and be safe with my rifle. But that didn't mean I didn't learn that lesson the hard way before it completely stuck with me.

After one hunting trip with my father, it was freezing out, too cold to stand outside and clear our rifles. I joined the rest of my family in the house. My mother was in the kitchen preparing dinner. My sisters were at the kitchen table playing a game.

I pulled off my gloves and started to clear my rifle. My father had taught me how to clear the chamber several times, emphasizing safety. First, take out the magazine and then work the action to eject any rounds before looking in the chamber and then dry firing in a safe direction into the ground.

On this particular occasion, I wasn't paying attention and I must have chambered a round, and then I slid the magazine out. Pointing the gun toward the floor, I took it off of safe and squeezed the trigger. The bullet exploded from the barrel and buried itself into the floor in front of the wood stove. I hadn't been paying attention because I was trying to warm up. The boom echoed throughout the house.

I froze.

My heart was beating so hard it hurt my chest. My hands were shaking. I looked at my father, who was looking at the tiny hole in the floor. My mother and sisters came running over to see what happened.

"You OK?" my father asked.

I stammered a yes and checked the rifle to make sure it was clear. With my hands still shaking, I put the rifle down.

"I'm sorry," I said. "I forgot to check the chamber."

I was more embarrassed than anything else. I knew how to handle my rifle, but I'd gotten careless because I was more focused on getting warm. My father cleared his own rifle and hung up his coat. He wasn't angry. He just wanted to make sure I knew what happened.

Kneeling down next to me with my rifle, we went through the steps again.

"What did you do wrong? Talk me through it," he said.

"Take the magazine out," I said. "Clear the chamber. Check it. Take it off of safe and pull the trigger in a safe direction."

I showed him how to clear it properly a couple of times, and then we hung the gun in the rack near the door. It takes only one time to screw things up. And I learned from it. It was a huge lesson, and I never forgot again.

Just like I never forgot another "moving, move" call after that day in the kill house.

Our daily schedule in Green Team during the CQB portion started at dawn. We worked out as a class each morning. Then, for the rest of the day, half of the thirty-man class would go to the range and the other half would go to the kill house. At lunch, we'd switch.

The ranges were some of the best in the world. This wasn't your basic range where you shot at targets from a line. No, we'd race through obstacles, fire from the skeletons of burnt-out cars, and do a set of pull-ups before racing to shoot a series of targets. We always seemed to be moving. We already had the basics down, we were learning to shoot in combat. The instructors worked to get our heart rates up so that we had to control our breathing while we shot.

Our training facility had two kill houses. One was made of stacked railroad ties. It had a few long hallways and basic square rooms. The newer house was modular and could be reconfigured to resemble conference rooms, bathrooms, and even a ballroom. We rarely saw the same layout more than once. The goal was to throw something new at us each day to see how we handled it.

The pace of training was fast. The instructors didn't wait for people to catch up. It was a speeding train, and if you didn't catch on by the first day, you would most likely be heading back to your previous unit in very short order. Like a reality show, each week our numbers grew smaller as guys washed out. It was all a part of preparing us for the real world, and ferreting out the "Gray Man." He was the guy who blended into the group. Never the best guy, but also not the worst, the Gray Man always met the standards, exceeding them rarely, and stayed invisible. To root out the Gray Man, the instructors gave us a few minutes at the end of the week to perform peer rankings.

We sat at beat-up picnic tables under an awning. The instructors gave each one of us a piece of paper.

"Top five, bottom five, gentlemen," one of the instructors said. "You've got five minutes."

We each had to make an anonymous list of the five best performers in the class and the five worst. The instructors didn't see us all hours of the day, so top-five-bottom-five allowed them to get a better sense of who was really performing well. A candidate could be a great shot and do everything perfectly in the kill house, but outside of training he wouldn't be easy to work with or live with. The instructors took our top-five-bottom-five and compared them with their lists. Our assessment contributed to the fate of a candidate because it drew a clearer picture of the student.

At the beginning, it was kind of obvious who the bottom five were in the class. It was easy to see the weak links. But as those guys started to disappear it wasn't so easy to pick the bottom five anymore.

Charlie was always in my top five. So was Steve. Like Charlie, Steve was an East Coast SEAL. I used to hang out with Steve and Charlie on the weekends and during our training trips.

If Steve wasn't working, he was reading, mostly nonfiction with an emphasis on current events and politics. He also had a decent stock portfolio, which he monitored on his laptop during the few hours of downtime. Not only was he an outstanding SEAL, he could talk politics, investing, and football at the same level.

He was thick, not lean like a swimmer but more like a linebacker. Charlie used to joke that Steve looked like a groundhog.

He was one of the few who routinely kicked my ass with a pistol. At the end of each day, I would always check his score to see if he beat me. Like Charlie, Steve had been a CQB instructor for the East Coast teams before coming to Green Team. He had three deployments, and he was one of the few East Coast guys with any combat experience. At that time, only West Coast teams had deployed to Iraq or Afghanistan. Steve had deployed to Bosnia in the late 1990s and his team got into a firefight, one of the few before September 11.

Charlie and Steve always seemed to end up on the top of my list. As more and more guys washed out, the task became harder and harder.

"Coming up with bottom five is kicking my ass," I said to Steve one night.

We were both sitting at the table in the range house cleaning our rifles.

"Who were your bottom five last week?" he said.

I rattled off some names, many of the same guys on Steve's list.

"I don't know who to put down this week," I said.

"Ever think of putting yourself down there?" Steve said.

"I got three names. The last two, I don't know," I said. "I guess we could use our own names. I don't want to throw someone else under the bus."

I didn't think either of us was doing badly in the class.

"I'm going to risk it," Steve said. "We need five names."

A few weeks earlier, we tried to leave the bottom five blank. As a class, we decided to rebel and stand up to the instructors. It didn't last long. We spent the rest of the night running and pushing cars for hours, instead of unwinding after a long day of training.

That Friday, I put my own name down on the bottom five. So did Steve. He was willing to stand up for what was right. Steve was a leader in the class, and when he came up with ideas, guys listened.

By the end of the CQB block of training in Mississippi, we had lost about a third of the class. The guys who washed out couldn't process information fast enough to make the correct split-second decision. It wasn't that they were bad guys, because a lot would re-screen and make it through on their second try. Those who didn't would go back to their regular teams, where they'd typically excel.

The rumor around the command was if you passed the CQB block of training, you had a more than fifty-fifty chance of passing Green Team. The instructors heard the same rumor, so when we got back to Virginia Beach, they kept the pressure on, never letting us forget that we were a very long way from being done.

We were only three months into a nine-month training course. The next six months wouldn't be any easier. After CQB, we went on to train on explosive breaching, land warfare, and communications.

One of the SEALs' core jobs is ship boarding, called "underways." We spent weeks practicing boarding a variety of boats from cruise ships to cargo vessels. Although we spent a lot of time in Afghanistan and Iraq, we needed to be proficient in the water. We rehearsed "over the beach" operations where we would swim through the surf zone and patrol over the beach and conduct a raid. Afterward, we'd disappear into the ocean, linking up with our boats offshore.

During the last month of training we practiced VIP security details. Afghan president Hamid Karzai's first security detail were SEALs from the command. We also attended an advanced course in SERE, or Survival Evasion Resistance and Escape.

The key to the course was managing stress.

The instructors kept everyone tired and on edge, forcing

us to make important decisions under the worst conditions. It was the only way the instructors could mimic combat. Success or failure of our missions was a direct reflection of how each operator could process information in a stressful environment. Green Team was different than BUD/S because I knew just passing the swim or run and being cold, all without quitting, wasn't enough.

Green Team was about mental toughness.

During this time we were also learning the culture of the command. Throughout Green Team, we were on a one-hour recall to simulate what we would experience on the second deck. If recalled, the pager buzzed and we had an hour to get back to work and check in. Every day at six o'clock, we got a test page. The pagers became another source of pressure the instructors used. Several times, we'd get pages before dawn to come into work.

One Sunday around midnight, my pager went off. Still shaking the sleep from my head, I rolled into the base in time and was told to put on my PT gear and stand by. We were going to have a PT test.

We weren't supposed to be more than an hour away and couldn't drink to intoxication. We had to be able to perform when called upon. We could get a page and be on a plane to anywhere in the world within hours.

Soon, my teammates started to arrive. Some seemed like the page had interrupted a trip to the bar.

"Are you drunk right now?" I heard an instructor ask another candidate.

"Of course not. I just had a beer at the house," he said.

As the hour ticked away, I still didn't see Charlie.

He rolled in about twenty minutes late. The instructors were pissed. He'd gotten a ticket for speeding on his way, which only delayed him more. Thankfully, it was just a verbal lashing from the instructors and Charlie was able to stay with our class.

With only weeks left in the nine-month training, we started to hear rumors about the draft. To fill out the squadrons, the instructors would rank the whole class and then assault squadron master chiefs would sit around a table and pick new members from my Green Team class.

The individual squadrons were in a constant state of flux as they rotated from deployments overseas to months of training and then months on standby, during which a call to deploy could come at any time.

After the draft, the Green Team instructors posted a list. A whole bunch of my friends, including me, Charlie, and Steve, were going to the same squadron.

"Hey, congrats," Tom said when he saw me looking at the list. "When I am done with my instructor time I am going back to that squadron to be a team leader."

SEALs are deployed around the world at any given time. The heart of each squadron are the teams, each led by a senior enlisted SEAL and made up of a half dozen operators apiece. The teams make up troops, which are led by a lieutenant commander. Multiple troops make up a squadron, led by a commander. DEVGRU assault squadrons are augmented by intelligence analysts and support personnel.

When you get to a team, you slowly work your way up the chain. Most of the time, you stay in the same team, unless you get tapped to be a Green Team instructor or work a collateral duty.

The day after the draft, I brought my gear up to the second deck. I followed Steve and Charlie to the squadron team room. The room was large, with a small bar and kitchen area in one corner. Everyone had brought a case of beer, a tradition when you show up at the squadron for the first time.

Our squadron was getting ready to go on standby and then deploy to Afghanistan. Some of my teammates from Green Team were already packing their gear and deploying as brand-new assaulters with their respective squadrons.

Along one wall, the commander and master chief had offices. A massive table took up most of the room, with smaller tables with computers along the perimeter. Flat-screens that were used in briefings hung on one wall. The rest of the wall space was filled with plaques from other units like the Australian SAS and mementos from past missions. A bloody hood and flex-cuffs were mounted on a plaque on the wall after the squadron captured a Bosnian war criminal in the 1990s. Petty Officer 1st Class Neil Roberts's Squad Automatic Weapon, or SAW, was also hung on the wall. He fell out of a Chinook helicopter after it was hit by two rocket-propelled grenades during Operation Anaconda in Afghanistan and was killed by Taliban fighters at the start of the war.

As we lined up at the head of the table, I saw all these senior guys with long hair and beards. Tattoos covered most of their arms, and only a few were in uniform. Toward the end of Green Team, we all started growing out our hair and beards. The grooming standards have changed several times over the years, but at this point in the war, people were less worried about your haircut and more worried about your actions on the battlefield. It was a ragtag bunch of professionals. We all came from different backgrounds and we had different hobbies and interests, but what we had in common was a willingness to sacrifice our time and even our lives for a greater good.

In the team room, the guys made us introduce ourselves and give them a brief bio. Charlie, the bully, was the first to speak and he barely got out his name before he was met with a chorus of boos and jeers from the senior guys.

"Shut up," they yelled. "We don't care."

It went that way for all of us. But afterward, the guys were shaking our hands and helping us get our gear unpacked. It was all in fun and, besides, everybody was too busy to worry about it. There was a war going on and no time to be wasted with petty new-guy treatment.

I felt at home.

This was the kind of command I'd wanted to be a part of since I joined the Navy. Here, there were no limits on how good you could be and what you could contribute. For me, all of the fear of failure was now replaced with the desire to perform and excel.

What I had learned during the three-day screening more than a year ago was even more true in the squadron: just meeting the standards wasn't good enough.

As I unpacked my gear, I realized I had to prove myself all over again. Just because I got through Green Team didn't mean shit. All of the other guys in the room completed the same course. I made a promise to myself that I would be an asset to the team and that I'd work my ass off.

CHAPTER 3

The Second Deck

A few weeks before we were scheduled to deploy to Afghanistan, I printed out the packing list. It was 2005 and I was preparing for my first deployment to the central Asian country. While at SEAL Team Five, my only combat deployment had been to Iraq. Standing next to the printer, I watched as the paper rolled out. Six single-spaccd pages later, I started to gather up my gear. The suggested packing list basically told us to bring everything.

We worked under "Big Boy Rules" at the command, which means there wasn't a lot of management unless you needed it. Since getting to the team, I prided myself on being independent. For the last three months, I had trained hard and tried to be an asset. I learned that it was OK to ask questions if you have them, but you didn't want to be the guy who didn't know what was going on and was always asking. I didn't want to make a mistake on my first deployment by not packing something, so when I saw my team leader in the team room I asked him about the packing list.

"Hey," I said, grabbing a cup of coffee. "I was getting my kit together and the packing list basically wants me to load everything."

He was sitting at the granite countertop sipping a cup of coffee and going over some paperwork. Short and stocky, unlike some of the other guys who had longer hair and thick beards, he was clean-cut, with a short haircut and a close shave. He also wasn't the most talkative guy and he had been at DEVGRU for much longer than I'd been in the Navy.

He took "Big Boy Rules" seriously.

"How long have you been in the Navy?" he said.

"Going on six years," I said.

"You've been a SEAL for six years, and you don't know what you need on deployment?"

I felt like an asshole.

"Dude, what do you think you need to bring for deployment? Load it," he said. "This is your guide. Bring what you think you need."

"Check," I said.

Back at my cage, I laid out my gear, called "kit." Each operator at DEVGRU had a cage, sort of like a locker big enough to walk inside. It was the size of a small room, with

42

shelves that lined the walls and a small hanging rod that ran along the back wall to hang uniforms.

Bags of gear filled with everything I needed for the different missions we could be called upon to perform rested on the shelves. One bag had everything I needed for CQB. Another had my HAHO (High Altitude, High Opening) or "jump gear." My combat swimmer or "dive kit" was in a separate large green gear bag. Everything was color-coded and ready. My OCD was definitely in overdrive, and I had everything perfectly organized and separated.

But some of the gear, like a Gerber tool, came in handy on most missions. Back at SEAL Team Five, you were issued one Gerber tool, which had a knife blade, screwdriver, scissors, and can opener.

You were also issued only one scope for your rifle.

One fixed blade knife.

One set of ballistic plates.

That meant sorting through multiple bags to find the single item that you needed to transfer to a new bag containing the specialty gear for a given mission. It was a hassle and was not very efficient, but it was the U.S. government and I'd gotten used to it.

But it was different at DEVGRU.

My team leader came by my cage later that day to double check how I was doing and saw my load-outs in the color-coded bags. Off to the side, I had an extra bag with the gear I thought I'd need for most missions, including a Gerber tool.

"Go down to supply and get a Gerber for each bag," my team leader said.

I looked at him confused.

"I can go get four of them?"

"Yeah, you got four different mission load-out bags. You need one Gerber for each bag," he said.

My team leader signed my request form and I walked down to the supply office. One of the support guys met me at the window.

"What do you need?"

I showed him the list. It was basic stuff like flashlights and other tools, but I wanted four of each.

"OK," he said without hesitation. "Be right back."

In a few minutes, he came back with a plastic bin full of everything on the list. I had to fight to keep from smiling too much. This was a dream come true. Back at our previous teams, guys spent thousands of their own dollars buying kit we needed for work.

The armory was even better. Above the door was a sign: "You dream, we build."

For a gun geek like me, it was heaven. I had them set up my two M4 assault rifles, one with a fourteen-inch barrel and one with a ten-inch barrel. I got an MP7 submachine gun and a collection of handguns, including the standard-issue Navy SEAL Sig Sauer P226. My primary weapon that I used daily was a suppressed Heckler & Koch (H&K) 416 with the ten-inch barrel and an EOTech optical red dot sight with a 3X magnifier. My H&K 416 with a fourteen-inch barrel I set up for long-range shooting. It was also suppressed, and on top I mounted a 2.5X10 Nightforce scope.

I also set up my fourteen-inch H&K 416 with an infrared laser and a clip-on thermal sight that allowed for more precise night shooting. I didn't use the gun much because my primary weapon, with the ten-inch barrel, worked for most missions, but it was nice to have a gun ready with a little more range if I needed it.

I ran with a suppressed MP7 submachine gun on a few missions, but it lacked the knockdown power of my H&K 416. The submachine gun came in handy during ship boarding, in the jungle, or when weight, size, and the ability to stay extremely quiet were needed. Several times we shot fighters in one room with a suppressed MP7 and their comrades next door didn't wake up. The H&K 416s didn't compare to the MP7 when you were trying to be extremely quiet.

Rounding out my guns were two pistols—the Sig Sauer P226 and an H&K 45C. Both were suppressor capable and I typically carried the 45. I also carried an M79 grenade launcher, which was called a pirate gun because it looked like a blunderbuss. Our armorers cut the barrel short and modified the stock into a pistol grip.

Of course, none of my guns were standard issue. We all had individual modifications on the trigger and grips. I know for a fact the armorers took great pride in taking care of the tools that took care of us. Without a doubt, DEVGRU had the best tools in the business.

As you walked around the command, it wasn't uncommon to hear rounds being shot at the indoor and outdoor ranges, or hear the thud of a breaching charge going off in the kill house. Training was constant. It wasn't unusual to see guys walking between training events dressed in full kit, with their loaded weapon slung in front of them. Everything was geared toward war-fighting or training for it.

I was just getting the hang of things at the squadron in 2005 when I found myself on a plane headed overseas to Afghanistan. At the time, our unit was focused on Afghanistan, and the Army's Delta Force was in Iraq.

Delta hit a rough patch that year and had taken several casualties in a short time. They requested additional assault-ers, and DEVGRU rogered up and my team was selected to go. My squadron didn't want my first deployment to be with Delta, so I spent some time acting as a floater working with my troop in Afghanistan. Given Delta's needs, I eventually left Afghanistan with two other SEALs and headed to Iraq to help out.

We got into Baghdad well after midnight. The ride from the helicopter pad was dark as we weaved through the de-serted streets of the Green Zone. It was summer and the hu-midity hung like a blanket over everything. Sitting in the bed of a pickup truck with our gear, the breeze felt good. Every-thing felt and smelled the same as my first combat deployment to Baghdad with Team Five in 2003.

We had arrived just after the invasion started. Our first mission was to secure the Mukatayin hydroelectric dam northeast of the Iraqi capital. Our chain of command was afraid retreating Iraqi forces might destroy the dam to slow the American advance.

The plan was simple. Based on our experience, which was zero, we planned to fly to the X, which is a tactic that means we insert directly onto the target, keeping speed and surprise in our favor. In this case the X was the dam, and once over the target in a helicopter, we planned to fast-rope into the courtyard. From there, we'd rush the main building and clear and secure it. Nearby, the GROM, Poland's special operations unit, would clear another cluster of buildings while another group of SEALs would secure the outer perimeter using two dune buggies.

After a few days of waiting for the weather to clear up, we got the word to go. Climbing into the MH-53, I could feel my heart beating quickly. I'd been waiting for this moment since I was a kid reading about ambushes in the Mekong Delta.

I was about to launch on my first real combat operation. I'd thought about it, read about it, and now here I was about to do it for real.

I probably should have been scared, or at least concerned about the unknown, but it felt good to finally do it for real. I didn't just want to practice the game, I wanted to actually play in the game, and this was going to be my first taste.

The flight took several hours and included a midair-refueling linkup. My team of twenty guys was crammed tightly inside the helicopter. The fuel smell wafted into the cabin as the helicopter filled its tanks using the boom in front of the cockpit. It was pitch-black inside the cabin, and I zoned out for most of the flight until we got the signal to get ready.

"Two minutes," the crew chief screamed, signaling with his hands and turning on a red light. It was well after midnight as the helicopter approached the dam.

I took my position at the door and grabbed the rope. I couldn't hear anything over the roar of the engines. Like the rest of my teammates, I was loaded down with breaching gear and our chemical protective suits. The "good idea fairy"— which is what we called the tendency for planners to add their two cents about every possible contingency, weighing the team down with options and extra gear and "good" ideas— had struck often on this mission. We were loaded down with quickie saws to break open the dam's gates. We had to carry food and water for a few days. We didn't know how long we'd be there, so we needed to be self-sufficient. The rule is, "When in doubt, load it out." Of course the more you carry, the greater a toll it takes on your body, the slower you move, the harder it is to react quickly to a threat.

As the helicopter slowed to a hover, I grabbed the rope with both hands and slid down to the ground. We were about thirty feet up, and I could see the ground coming quickly. I tried to slow my descent, but I didn't want to be so slow that my teammates would crash down on top of me. With all my gear, I landed like a ton of bricks. My legs ached as I brought my gun up and started toward the gate less than one hundred yards away.

As soon as I stepped out from under the helicopter, the rotor wash beat me down. Small rocks pelted my body and dust tore at my eyes. I could barely make out the gate ahead of me. As I started to run toward it, the rotor wash pushed me forward into an uncontrolled sprint. It took every effort to stay on my feet, and I literally skidded to a halt at the locked gate.

The others were close behind me. I snapped the lock off the gate with my bolt cutters, then took point and headed toward a cluster of buildings. The main building was two stories and had the drab architecture of an Eastern-bloc country, made of concrete, and the door was metal. While my teammates covered me, I tried the handle. It was open.

I didn't know what I would find as I stepped into a long hall. We could start taking fire at any second.

I could see several rooms on either side. As we started to move forward, we saw movement in one of the far rooms. Two hands came out first, followed by several Iraqi guards. They had their hands above their heads and they were unarmed.

My teammates ushered them behind me as I continued down the hall. Inside the rooms, I found their AK-47 rifles. None of the weapons had a round in the chamber. It looked like they'd been sleeping and had woken when they heard the helicopters overhead.

It took a long time to clear the building because of the size. We paid special attention to detail because we were looking for explosives rigged to blow up the dam. We'd never cleared anything this size, so it took a little longer than expected.

No one was injured except for one of the GROM guys who broke his ankle fast-roping to the target.

After we cleared the main building, my platoon chief came up to me.

"Hey, check my radio," he said. "I am not getting comms."

When we launched, he had his radio strapped to his back. As he stood in front of me now, I could still see the headphone cord dangling over his shoulder. I looked on his back and the whole pack was gone. All I could see was the cable.

"Your backpack is gone," I said.

"Gone? What do you mean?" he said.

"It's gone," I said.

He hadn't strapped the backpack to his body armor correctly. Body armor has nylon loops about a half-inch apart on the front and back so that you can secure pouches to the vest. My chief had only laced his backpack through the top and bottom loops, so when he fast-roped down into the rotor wash, it blew his backpack and radio off his back and into the water below the dam. The radio at the bottom of the river wasn't going to do us much good. The same thing happened to our medic. He lost a bunch of morphine in a similar backpack.

A lot of the gear we were using on the mission was new to us. Just before we deployed, boxes of new stuff had shown up in the team room. The common mantra was "Train like you fight," which means don't go into battle with equipment you haven't used before, preferably extensively. We'd broken that rule, and I knew we'd gotten extremely lucky that it didn't bite us in the ass. It was our first lesson learned.

That wasn't the only way we were lucky on the mission. The Iraqis had antiaircraft guns near the dam loaded and ready. Had the guards wanted to fight, they could have knocked the helicopters out of the sky as we fast-roped down.

We learned a million lessons on that mission, from the need for better intelligence about a target to how to secure equipment, and we'd learned them all without losing anybody. Usually the best lessons are learned at the toughest moments, but I didn't like how much luck had played a role in keeping us alive on that mission, and my perfectionist tendencies took an ego hit.

As the helicopter took off to take us back to Kuwait three days later, I realized that even though each of my teammates on Team Five had different amounts of time and experience in the SEAL teams, we were all still very new to this, and this raid was a first for everyone.

Delta

Now back in Baghdad two years later, I was a little more seasoned, but not much. I'd screened for and then completed Green Team, but I was definitely still the new guy. The good part was I had some experience working in the Iraqi capital from my days on Team Five. After the dam mission, my team was sent to Baghdad to help round up former regime loyalists and insurgent leaders.

Delta's base was in the Green Zone, which sat next to the Tigris River in the center of the city. Soon after I landed, I started to immediately get my bearings. The base was a short distance from the famed crossed swords, erected to celebrate Iraq's "victory" in the Iran-Iraq war. The sword arch stood on

opposite sides of a large parade ground. During the day, you'd
see whole units posing for pictures near the pair of hands
holding the curved blades. The hands and forearms were mod-
eled on the dictator's, including his exact thumb print.

Delta's headquarters was in former Baath Party buildings. I walked inside to check in at the Joint Operations
Center. Jon, my new team leader, came up to meet me soon
after I arrived. I was brand-new and still had no idea what to
expect.

A former Ranger before joining Delta Force, Jon had a
thick barrel chest and thick arms. A brown bushy beard that
was so long it brushed against the top of his chest covered his
face. He looked like a taller version of Gimli, the angry dwarf
in *The Lord of the Rings*.

Jon had joined the Army right out of high school. After
years of short haircuts and lots of rules with the Rangers, he
dropped his packet for warrant officer school with an eye
toward being an Apache helicopter pilot. But, ultimately, he
didn't want to give up his gun. So he screened and got picked
up for Delta and had worked his way up the ranks.

"Welcome to paradise," he said, as we walked toward the
team room. "Hot enough for you?"

"At least you guys have AC," I said. "Last time I was here,
I lived in a tent. We didn't get AC for weeks."

"A little better living here," he said, opening the door to
our room.

The room was in one wing of the palace. The hallways
were wide, with marble floors and high ceilings. I was going to

share a room with him and the newest guy on their team. My bunk bed was in the near corner, and I tossed my bags next to it. Jon helped me wheel my gear into the room before showing me around the palace.

The palace had its own gym, chow hall, and pool. In fact, there was more than one pool. Each team had two rooms. There were five guys on the team. One of them was a former British Royal Marine who had dual citizenship. He came to the United States, enlisted, and eventually worked his way into the ranks of Delta. The other guys were like Jon, a mix of former Rangers and Special Forces soldiers. The newest guy was a Ranger who was wounded in Somalia during the "Black Hawk Down" battle. He looked like an Amish guy with a bowl haircut and a patchy beard that never seemed to grow together.

After making small talk, I spent the rest of the night getting my gear in order. First, I unpacked my "op gear" in a cubby in the hallway outside of the room so that if something went down, I'd be able to throw on our gear and be out the door. After that was squared away, I unpacked my clothes and set up my bed. Since we had bunk beds, most of us used the top bunk for storage and hung a poncho liner over the bottom so we had a little privacy.

It was close to dawn when I was finally done. Since we worked vampire hours—sleep all day and work at night—most of the guys were racking out. The room had a couch and a TV. I grabbed a cup of coffee and was watching TV when Jon came over.

"We'll get you plugged in tomorrow," Jon said. "Let me know when you need anything."

"Thanks," I said.

"We've been busy," Jon said. "This was a rare day off. I'm sure we'll be out tomorrow night."

There was no easing into it. Most days, I'd get up in the afternoon and wander out to the pool with my iPod speakers. I'd chill to some Red Hot Chili Peppers or Linkin Park while I stretched out on an air mattress. I'd float a while, getting some sun and relaxing. One of my teammates started to take care of the grass around the pool as a hobby. In a country of sand and dirt, having a little grass to walk on was a real treat. Some days, I could smell fresh cut grass as I floated.

Then I'd eat breakfast and work out in the gym or run. I tried to get to the range as many times a week as possible. By dusk, missions would start spinning up and we'd knock out one operation, two if we were lucky.

I was part of the "roof team," which meant we rode on pods above the skid on an MH-6 Little Bird. We would land on the roof of a target compound and then assault down. The rest of the force would arrive in armored vehicles and clear the ground floor and assault up.

The Little Bird is a light helicopter used for special operations in the United States Army. It has a distinct egglike cockpit and two pods or bench seats on the outside. On the "attack" variant, the pods or seats are replaced with rockets and machine guns.

Pilots from the 160th Special Operations Aviation Regiment (SOAR) flew the helicopters. The 160th Special Operations Aviation Regiment flies most of the missions for JSOC. We've worked together for years and the 160th pilots are the best in the world. Headquartered at Fort Campbell, Kentucky, the 160th SOAR (Airborne) are known as the Night Stalkers, because almost all of their missions are done at night.

I'd worked with Little Birds briefly in Green Team, but in Baghdad I found myself perched on the skid almost every night as the city passed underneath me in a blur.

It was past midnight a few nights after I arrived, and all I could hear was the roar of the engine and the wind. At seventy miles per hour, the wind battered me as my feet dangled off the side of the seat. I knew calm, clear decision-making was the key. But that was hard when it felt like I was riding a roller coaster into a fight.

I tightened the sling on my gun, keeping it pinned to my chest, and checked the safety lanyard that would hopefully keep me attached to the helicopter in the event I slid off my seat. Sitting on the pod, I could see the other Little Bird on our right flank flying in formation in the green hue of my night vision goggles. From the other helicopter, one of the Delta guys saw me looking and flipped me the bird. I returned the salute.

On this hit, we were after a high-level weapons facilitator, just another link in the chain funding the insurgency. He was holed up in a cluster of two-story houses near the center of the city with several fighters and a large weapons cache. Our team was tasked with flying via Little Bird to the roof and assaulting down. Another team would come via a Pandur, an armored truck with .50 caliber machine guns and Mark 19 grenade launchers. They'd wait about half a minute for us to breach the roof door, creating a diversion, before they would breach the bottom floor and we'd clear our way to the middle.

Below me, the city stretched out in a tangle of roads and alleyways built around clusters of squat buildings. Every once in a while, the city would open up into an abandoned lot choked with trash. I was at the front of the pod near the cockpit. On the opposite side was Jon.

"One minute," I heard the pilot say over my radio. He calmly pointed a single finger out his door and in front of my face to make sure I got the call.

From my position, I could see the copilot pointing a laser at the roof of the target. Night after night, the pilots managed to navigate to the exact rooftop through a sea of thousands. I had no idea how they did it, since everything looked the same to me from above.

I could feel the helicopter start to descend toward the empty rooftop. Coming to a hover, the pilot was able to perform a lip landing by placing the skids on the edge of the rooftop. Instead of fast-roping, we stepped onto the skid and then jumped to the roof. In less than ten seconds, the whole four-man team was on the roof and the Little Bird was gone.

Racing to the door, the breacher set our charge and blew it open. Seconds later, I heard the charge blow on the first floor followed by shots being fired.

Jon was up front as we started down the stairs.

"We're on the wrong roof," Jon said, only a few steps inside.

The shooting was coming from the house next door. I heard several small explosions that had to be hand grenades as we ran to the corner of the roof.

"We're one building too far," Jon said. We moved to see how we could support our teammates in the building next door.

The houses looked the same from the air and for the first time the pilots had inserted us on the wrong one. We had approached from the south and landed on the building just to the north of our target.

"We need to move to the adjacent building," Jon said. "We're not useful staying here."

The adjacent building was east of the target and three stories tall, which allowed us to cover down at the target house.

"We've got an eagle down," I heard over the radio. That meant someone had been hit.

It turned out one of the Delta operators was shot in the calf. Others had been peppered with shrapnel from the hand grenades.

Insurgents in the house were throwing grenades down the stairwell, slowing the operators' advance as they finished clearing the first floor and moved toward the second.

The ground team started to work a medevac, and pulled back away from the stairs. We were able to race around the block and clear the three-story building to the east of the target.

Explosions and gunfire echoed through the buildings. From the roof of the building, we started to scan for targets. I could see IR lasers tracking over the windows of the compound as my teammates looked for targets. Every few minutes, one of the insurgents would stick an AK-47 out of the second-floor window and unleash a long burst.

"*Allahu Akbar*," they'd scream after spraying rounds down at the assaulters below.

It was a stalemate. The team on the ground couldn't run up the stairs, and there was no way we could get on the roof to fight down. Over the radio, I heard calls to an Army mechanized infantry unit ten blocks away. The soldiers were providing the outer ring of security.

We always liked to have two rings of security. This night, the near ring was a squad of Rangers, who set up on the corners of the target area. A mile beyond that were M1 tanks and Bradley Fighting Vehicles, which were armored personnel carriers with a 20mm turret gun.

"Bring up a Bradley," I heard over the radio.

I could hear the Bradley's tracks chewing up the asphalt as it approached the house.

"I want you to level the second floor," the assault leader yelled to the Bradley's commander perched in the hatch on top of the turret.

Smashing through a stone wall on the south side of the house, it stopped in the courtyard and unleashed a short burst from its 20mm cannon. The rounds easily smashed through the walls of the second floor, tearing large gashes in the concrete.

Pulling back, I saw the assault leader run up to the Bradley.

"Keep shooting," the commander yelled into the hatch.

"What?" the gunner said.

"I want you to level the whole second floor," the assault leader repeated. "Level it."

The Bradley crunched back over the rubble again and started to fire. One of the insurgents screamed *"Allahu Akbar!"* and started to spray bullets out the window.

This time, there was no letup from the Bradley. Guys started to cheer as the rounds hit in successive explosions. In a few minutes, the Bradley went Winchester, which is the military term for running out of ammunition. We brought up a second Bradley and it shot until it went Winchester as well.

By the time the second Bradley pulled back, a raging fire had erupted on the second floor. Black smoke poured out of the windows and started to billow into the sky. From our position on the roof, we could still hear the insurgents yelling. I was perched on the northeast corner, holding down on the backside of the house. It was hard to see because of the thick black smoke.

Suddenly, I saw a man's head and torso emerge from a window.

Without thinking, I put my laser on his chest and opened fire. I could see the bullets hit him and he flopped back into the room, disappearing into the smoke.

After my volley of fire, Jon raced over beside me.

"What you got?"

"Saw a guy in the back window," I said.

"You sure?" he said, scanning the same window with his laser.

"Yeah."

"You get him?"

"Pretty sure," I said.

"OK. Stay put."

Jon went back to his post and I kept searching for new targets. I didn't have time to dwell on it nor did I have any feelings about it. This was the first person I'd ever shot and with all the time I'd spent thinking about how it would make me feel, it really didn't make me feel anything. I knew that these guys in the house had already tried to kill my friends on the first floor and they wouldn't hesitate to do the same to me.

Even after the two Bradleys and the fire, we still heard yelling followed by bursts of enemy fire. Tactically, it didn't make sense to assault up the stairs.

"They're going to blow the building," Jon said.

Jon decided to pull us off the roof rather than expose us to the blast. We joined the others on the ground. I watched as a small breach team, led by one of Delta's Explosive Ordnance Disposal guys, ran into the first floor to set a thermobaric charge. The charge produces a huge shock wave capable of collapsing an entire building.

A few minutes later, the charge was set and the breach team ran back and took cover next to me. Hunkered behind the Pandur, I could hear him counting down. I waited for the explosion.

Nothing.

Everybody stared at the EOD tech. We all had the same confused look on our faces. I saw Jon walk toward him.

"What the hell?" Jon said.

"The time must have been wrong," I heard him mumble.

I am sure his mind was running a million miles an hour. He was trying to figure out why the charge didn't blow.

"Did you dual prime?" Jon asked.

Everybody was trained to dual prime explosives, which meant attaching two detonators to the charge in case one fails. The rule of thumb was simple: One is none. Two is one.

But that didn't help us now. We had to make a decision. Do we send more guys back into the house to reset the charge, or do we wait it out and see what happens? We had no idea if the insurgents moved downstairs and were now waiting for the assaulters to return, or if the EOD set the wrong time and it would go off unexpectedly with men inside.

Finally, they decided to send the EOD tech back inside to attach a new detonator. Again, the breach team ran back inside. We continued to cover the house, and minutes later the breach team was back behind the Pandur.

"You think it is going to go this time?" Jon asked with a smirk.

"Yeah, I am pretty positive," the EOD tech said. "Dual primed it."

On time, the charge exploded and the house crumbled onto itself, sending out a massive cloud covering us in thin, talc-like dust. I watched the cloud rise into the sky and hang in the muggy morning air. By now, the sun was starting to come up.

We moved in to sift through the rubble looking for bodies and weapons. There were at least six dead fighters. Most of the bodies were up on the second floor. Their faces were covered in soot. Jon noticed the sandbags near some of the bodies.

"Hey, look at this. They had the whole second floor barricaded," he said. "We're lucky the pilots made a mistake. It probably saved our lives."

"Why?" I asked.

"If we'd actually landed on the right building," Jon said, "the four of us would have assaulted into a barricaded position on the second floor. We might have had surprise on our side, but the odds wouldn't have looked good once we made entry. Without a doubt in my mind, we would have taken more casualties."

I was quiet. I looked up to Jon and here he was saying we were lucky. A mistake had probably saved our lives. It was nothing but a bit of random luck.

After clearing the rubble, the ride back to the base in the Pandurs was quiet. We were hungry and tired. All of our faces were covered in soot. Usually there was more smack talking and excitement after taking down such a dynamic target. I let what happened start creeping into my mind.

As we rode, Jon's words kept echoing in my head. Had the

mission gone perfectly, we would have landed the Little Bird on the roof and entered the door on the second floor, only to come face-to-face with at least four heavily armed insurgents. A four-on-four gunfight with automatic weapons in a room no bigger than a bedroom never ends well.

By the time we parked back at our base, I had finished my mental gymnastics. I simply blocked out what could have happened and moved on to what I learned: Sometimes something random can save your life. And always dual prime a charge.

At the end of the deployment, I flew back to Pope Air Force Base in North Carolina, where Delta is based. When we got off the plane, members of their unit greeted me just like I was one of their own.

Before I boarded my flight to Virginia Beach, Jon handed me a plaque. It was a copy of a pencil drawing of a Delta operator and a Little Bird. It was framed with green matting and a Delta Force unit coin.

"I want you to have this," Jon said. "Anybody who runs with this team gets one."

Master Sergeant Randy Shughart, a Delta sniper, made the drawing, and the original was found after he was killed in Somalia. Shughart was awarded the Medal of Honor during the Battle of Mogadishu. When the Black Hawk crashed, he volunteered to defend the crash site until help arrived. He was killed by a mob of Somalis.

Before the attacks on September 11, Delta and DEVGRU were rivals. We were the two kids at the top of the block, and there was a raging debate over which unit was the best. With the war, there was no more time for rivalry and all that bullshit had gone away. They treated me like a brother during the deployment.

I shook hands with Jon and boarded my flight to Virginia Beach.

Back home at DEVGRU the next day, I met up with Charlie and Steve. They came over to my cage while I unpacked and got my gear back in its proper place. The squadron was just returning from its deployment in Afghanistan. Compared to my trip to Baghdad, their deployment had been relatively slow.

As much fun as I had in Iraq with Delta, it was still good to be back with the boys.

"Sounds like you were busy over there," Charlie said.

"When are you moving down to Bragg with your Army brothers?" Steve said.

My jokes were weak, and I knew they were talking shit. It was great to be back.

"Ha-ha," I said. "Good to see you guys too."

I was looking forward to leave and then a trip to Mississippi to shoot. I knew the only chance I had to shut them up was on the range. Even though we'd all just gotten home, we weren't scheduled to stay long. Two weeks of leave is all we had before heading out to train. It was a cycle we would repeat for almost a decade.

CHAPTER 5

Point Man

In December 2006, we were deployed to western Iraq. It was my third deployment at the command. I had spent one rotation working closely with the CIA. It felt good to be back with the guys instead of helping the agency plan and train their Afghan fighters. We worked with a lot of other units, but it was always better with the boys because we were cut from the same cloth.

My troop was working along the Syrian border and in some of Iraq's nastiest towns like Ramadi, home to al Qaeda Iraq. Our job was to target high-level couriers that brought in foreign fighters and Iranian weapons.

The Marines in Al Anbar asked if we could help conduct an

operation to clear and secure a series of houses in a village near the Syrian border. The village was a safe haven for insurgents, and several leaders were staying near the center of the town. The plan was for us to hit the houses at night and then the Marines would surround the village and relieve us in the morning.

Even with the team crowded into a Black Hawk, I was fighting to keep warm.

We had a combat assault dog with us. We used it to detect bombs and help track enemy fighters. I tried to get the dog to sit on my lap to warm me up. Every time I got him close to me, the handler would pull him away.

It was freezing when we landed about four miles from the Iraqi village. Shielding my eyes from the dust, I waited for the helicopters to leave. I could hear their engines fade away minutes later, heading east back toward Al Asad Air Base.

I stamped my feet and rubbed my hands together trying to get the circulation moving while we got organized to move out.

Even though I'd been to Iraq twice before, this third deployment was different. The enemy had evolved. So, like SEALs do best, we adapted. Instead of flying to the X like we did in the past, we'd started to land miles away and patrol in quietly. This way the enemy couldn't hear the helicopters. We were transitioning from being loud and fast, taking the enemy by surprise, to being soft and slow and retaining the element of surprise for even longer. We could creep through their houses and into their bedrooms and wake them up before they had a chance to fight back.

But patrolling to the target wasn't easy, especially in the cold winter night. The wind cut into our uniforms as we moved toward the village. I was near the front, acting as the point man for my team.

One of the key lessons learned early on in a SEAL's career was the ability to be comfortable being uncomfortable. It was a lesson I first learned as a kid in Alaska checking the trap line with my dad.

When it got cold in Iraq or during Hell Week in BUD/S, my mind used to wander back to Alaska. I could always hear the roar of the snowmobile as my father and I headed toward the line of traps he kept miles from the village and deep into Alaska's wilderness.

I remember how it felt like the snowmobile was floating through the fresh powder, and how as we turned it was like being on a surfboard cutting into a wave. The temperature hovered near zero, and our warm breath crystallized in the air.

On one cold winter day in Alaska, I was wrapped tightly in a tan Carhartt snowsuit, winter boots, and gloves. A beaver hat hand-sewn by my mother covered my ears and a scarf protected my face, leaving only my eyes exposed. I was warm except for my hands and feet. We'd been out for hours and I could barely feel my toes.

I tried to wiggle them in my thick wool socks, but it wasn't helping. Huddled behind my father to block the wind, all I could think about was how cold my hands and feet were. We'd already gotten a couple of marten, a cat-size weasel with a bushy tail like a squirrel and a soft coat of brown fur. My father traded the pelts in the village to make a little extra money or my mother would make hats for my sisters.

But the biting cold took the thrill out of the time I was spending with my dad. Any fun I was having disappeared with the last feeling of warmth in my body.

I'd begged my father to go on the trip.

"Are you sure?" he said. "You know it is going to be cold."

"I want to go," I said.

I wanted to hang out with my father and didn't want to be stuck back at the house. This was guy stuff, and he taught me how to shoot and hunt. As I got older, he trusted me to hunt and fish on my own, and I'd take the family boat up the river for a week at a time. In a way, it was my first taste of "Big Boy Rules" and I thrived. Plus, I wouldn't have to sit at home with the girls.

I always wanted to be outside. I loved the outdoors, just not all the cold weather. I knew that if my dad let me come with him I couldn't be the kid complaining about the cold. But now, a few hours into the trip, all I wanted were warm hands and feet.

"Dad," I screamed into the wind as we drove. "Dad, my feet are frozen."

My father, dressed in the same snowsuit and hat, slowed to a stop. He turned back and I imagine he saw a small boy with his teeth chattering behind his scarf.

"I'm freezing," I said.

"We only have a few more traps," my father said. "Do you think you can make it?"

I just looked at him, not wanting to answer no. I didn't want to let him down. I stared at him hoping he'd make the choice for me.

"I can't feel my feet," I said.

"Get off here and start walking behind the snowmobile. Follow my tracks. I am going to keep going. I won't be far ahead of you. Stick to the tracks and keep moving because that will keep your feet warm."

I slid off the back of the snow machine and adjusted the .22 rifle strapped to my back.

"You got it?" my father asked.

I nodded.

He started the engine and headed toward the next trap. I started walking and my feet warmed up.

Outdoorsmen pay thousands of dollars to experience the Alaska tundra, but for most of my childhood all I had to do was walk outside my door.

My family had a sense of adventure not found in most people. When I was five years old, we moved to a small Eskimo village in the interior of Alaska. My parents were missionaries who met in college in California and found that their faith not only allowed them to spread Christianity but also appealed to their sense of adventure.

Besides his missionary work, my father worked for the state. The job required a college degree, and my father was one of the few people in the village that had one.

My mother stayed home with us. She helped with homework and kept my sisters and me on track. I was the middle child between two sisters. We were a tight family because there wasn't a lot to do in the village. Winters were brutal, so we'd huddle around the kitchen table and play board games.

But calling it a town by normal standards would be generous. We had two stores, together no bigger than a small truck stop, a small school, and a post office. No mall. No movie theater, but you could rent movies at one of the stores. The crown jewel of my town was the runway. It was just large enough to land a 737 jet as well as some of the bigger propeller-driven cargo planes. That made our village the hub of the region. Bush planes would come in and out of town bringing hunters and outdoorsmen from Anchorage to the more remote villages spread along the river.

We lived in a two-story house one hundred yards off the river. The house had a beautiful view of picturesque Alaska. Sometimes when I was lucky, I could see a moose or a bear from my front door. If I wasn't in school, I was out hunting or fishing. From the time I was a little kid, I was comfortable using a gun and moving in the woods, and being responsible for myself.

During BUD/S training, I excelled at land warfare. It was really no different than my hunting trips as a kid. With varying backgrounds at BUD/S, guys were stronger in different areas. I did fine in the water too, but I felt most comfortable during the weapons and land warfare training.

So, when I got to DEVGRU, I typically acted as the point man for my assault team. On this cold night in Iraq, the four-mile patrol to the target village took about an hour. It was close to three A.M. when we arrived. As we got close, I could see the lights from the Iraqi village flickering across a highway.

It was a dusty shit hole.

Light blue plastic shopping bags blew down the street. The smell of raw sewage from a ditch that ran along the road hung on the wind. I could just make out the biscuit-colored houses, which had a faint green hue under my night vision goggles. The power lines that ran along the highway into Syria sagged. Everything looked ratty and run down.

As we got to the village, the teams started to peel off to their predetermined targets. I led my team to our target building. Creeping up to the gate, I tried the handle. The heavy black iron door creaked open. Pushing it just wide enough to see in, I scanned the courtyard. It was empty.

The front door of the two-story house had a large window covered by an ornate grate. I could see inside the foyer as my teammates' lasers searched inside from the first-floor windows.

I slowly pushed open the front door of the house. It was unlocked. I paused at the threshold, my rifle at the ready, and waited. Looking over my shoulder, one of my teammates gave me a thumbs-up. I blinked the dust out of my eyes to make sure I could see before stepping inside. I was wearing my cumbersome op gear over a winter jacket as I tried to move like a cat.

"Think quiet," I told myself.

The foyer was cramped. A small generator sat on the floor. There was a door straight ahead of me and another door to my right. Ignoring the door to the right because it was blocked by a generator, I crept through the door in front of me.

My senses were on fire. I strained to hear any movement up ahead as I scanned the empty room. The smell of kerosene from the family's heating stove attacked my nostrils.

Every step that I took seemed like a huge crash. We were trained to anticipate an insurgent with a suicide vest or an AK-47 behind any door, ready to attack.

Curtains covered the doorway leading back to the bedrooms. I hated the curtains because at least with a door you felt a little protected. I had no idea if someone was looking under the curtain or was just waiting for my shadow to pass in front so that he could shoot.

This was the endgame. There was no way these rooms would be empty. We had no idea if the occupants had heard us. On my previous deployment with Delta, several of their guys were killed when they entered a house and got ambushed by a fighter hiding behind a sandbag wall. It was a deadly lesson we never forgot and it was always in the back of our minds as we entered a target.

I paused for a second or two, hoping to draw out any impatient ambushers. The light was on in the room behind the curtain. Flipping my night vision goggles up, I slowly pulled the curtain aside.

A long, slender refrigerator stood at the elbow of an L-shaped hallway. I spotted a door ajar and moved to quickly cover it while my teammates flooded the hallway, clearing the other rooms. One of my teammates followed me as we pushed open the door and cleared into a bedroom. There was no talking. Everyone knew his job.

Three mattresses were on the floor and I could barely make out two eyes staring at me from the corner of the dark room. It was a young man with wispy facial hair and dark eyes. He seemed nervous and his eyes kept shifting from side to side as we moved inside.

It struck me as odd that he just sat there staring at me.

There were two women, also awake, staring at the door. I immediately started moving toward the man. I knew something wasn't right because men usually sleep in a different room. As I passed the women, I held my hand out, waving at them to be calm. The man started to try and talk.

"SHHHH!" I whispered. I didn't want him to alert any men who might be in another room.

His gaze never left me. I grabbed him by his right arm and yanked him up, pushing the blankets away to make sure he didn't have a weapon. Holding him against the wall, I pulled the blankets off the women. Sleeping between the women was a small girl, no more than five or six years old. When I moved the blanket off of her, the girl's mother grabbed her and pulled her close.

I guided the man into the center of the room and secured his hands together with flex-cuffs—plastic handcuffs—and slid a hood over his head. My teammate watched the women while I quickly searched the man's pockets. I then pushed the man to his knees and shoved his head into the corner. He tried to talk, but I pressed his face against the wall, muffling his voice.

Our troop chief, who was running the mission, popped his head in the door.

"What do you have?" he said.

"One MAM," I said, which is shorthand for "military-aged male." "Still need to search the room."

I walked to the far corner of the room, next to the mattresses, and saw the brown stock of an AK-47. Resting on a pile of small plastic bags was a green chest rack, used to carry extra magazines, and a grenade.

"Got an AK over here," I said. "Chest rack. Grenade. FUCK!" I was pissed we hadn't seen the weapons earlier.

My teammate who covered the women hadn't seen them either when we came into the room.

The man I found in the room was definitely a fighter and a smart one too. He hid his gun, chest rack, and hand grenades just out of reach and well enough for us not to see them on our initial entry into the room.

Everything inside me wanted to shoot this guy right there on the spot. He knew the rules we had to follow and he was using them against us. We couldn't shoot him unless he posed a threat. If he had any balls, he would have lit us up coming through the door. He knew we were in the house. The man must have heard us come in and thought he could hide with the women.

With the house secure, I led the man to another room to

question him. The room's floor was covered in rugs, and sleeping mats were piled in a heap in the center of the room. A TV on the floor was on, but the screen was just static. Our interpreter stood next to the man as I pulled the hood off. His face was sweaty and his eyes were big as he tried to adjust to the light.

"Ask him why he had grenades and a chest rack," I told the interpreter.

"I'm a guest here," the man said.

"Why were you sleeping with the women and children? Guests don't sleep next to the women."

"One of them is my wife," he said.

"But I thought you were a guest here," I said.

The questioning went on like that for about a half hour. He never got his story straight and the next morning we turned him over to the Marines.

It was frustrating because missions were like this day after day. It was a catch and release system. We'd roll them up and in a few weeks the fighters would be back on the street. I was confident the fighter we found in the bedroom would be released soon. The only way to permanently take them off the street was if they were dead.

We found out later from some of the village elders that the men, including the fighter I encountered in the women's bedroom, were part of an insurgent cell that rotated between the houses of the village. The guy we captured had gone home that night to stay with his family. Three other guys in his cell were killed that same night after a short firefight with my teammates. My teammates got lucky and got the jump on them before the insurgents reacted. Our troop uncovered guns, mines, and explosives for roadside bombs in the house.

After clearing our initial targets, our troop searched the majority of the houses in the village. In one of the bedrooms, I found a pile of bras in one of the drawers. I fished out a nice white one with lace and a bow at the center. Balling it up, I stuffed it into the cargo pocket in my pants for later.

Outside, the BOP, BOP, BOP of the Marines' massive CH-53 helicopters echoed over the village. The sun was coming up as we held security positions in a nearby house. It was freezing. Mornings always seemed to be the coldest part of the day.

I looked up in time to see what looked like two big gray school buses fly over me, make a ninety-degree turn, and settle into the open desert just north of the power lines. The ramps in the back dropped down and out came the Marines just like you've seen in their commercials.

My troop chief walked past me to coordinate with the Marines so we could turn over the village and go home.

"You see their HQ?" he said.

"I think they are down the road," I said, pointing toward a cluster of men and radio antennas.

As he passed by, I fished out the bra from earlier that night and discreetly draped it on a radio antenna attached to his back. When it was cold and miserable it is the little things that warm you up. As he passed some of the Marines, I saw them stare at him and laugh.

"Hey, where is your HQ?" the troop chief asked a nearby Marine.

He pointed down the road.

"Hey, sir, you've got a bra hanging off your back," the Marine said.

"Yeah, I am sure there is," the troop chief said without hesitation, glancing back in our direction. "Happens all the time."

On the patrol back to the landing zone in the desert, I noticed something in my periphery vision blowing in the wind. Reaching back, I pulled on a bra strap.

Someone had hung a bra on the bolt cutters I had strapped to my back.

Pranks on the team were a way of life.

The pranking was so frequent that the squadron eventually built a wire diagram connecting all the suspected culprits. We used this same wire diagram to track terrorists. We had the names of all the guys in a pyramid with the worst prankster on top: Phil, my team leader at the time.

Phil had been in the Navy forever. He graduated Green Team the year I graduated BUD/S, left DEVGRU for a break, and joined the Leap Frogs, the Navy's parachute demonstration team. He also served as a military free-fall instructor before returning to the command.

I met Phil during my first days at the squadron and instantly liked him. He did several tours as an assaulter, then headed up the squadron's combat assault dog program before becoming my team leader.

Phil was a great prankster, maybe the best. At least once, I came back to my cage and found the shoelaces on all of my boots for my right foot cut. I couldn't prove Phil did it. I knew he had large magnets, which he'd wave over your wallet to demagnetize the strip on your credit card. He was famous for bombing all of your gear with glitter. I don't know how many pouches and uniforms I had to replace because purple glitter was caked on the Velcro or trapped in the folds of the fabric.

When things got slow, he'd create a feud.

"All right, who pranked me?" he would yell, walking into the team room.

But we all knew he pranked himself. He was trying to stir up a war because he was bored.

Sometimes, the guys did get him back. One Friday night after work, we all walked to the parking lot to find Phil's car high in the air. One of his victims, and it was never clear who, picked up his car with a forklift and left it there.

One of the longest running pranks in the squadron started with Phil. When we weren't deployed, we trained all over the United States. On this night, we were in Miami doing some urban training. It was just getting dark, and we were scheduled to practice CQB in an old abandoned hotel.

Before we started training, Phil and the local police, who kept onlookers away, went in to make sure it was empty. We didn't want to start training and run up on some homeless squatter. At the time, Phil was still working as a dog handler.

As they walked the halls, Phil glanced into a room and saw something sticking out of the drywall. It was a giant twelve-inch black dildo. Sliding a rubber glove on, Phil pulled it out of the wall and carried it downstairs.

"Look what I found," he said, waving it over his head.

"Get that thing away from me," I said, backing away as it flopped back and forth in his hand.

With the hotel clear, we started to train. It was just before dawn when we finished. After I put my kit into the trunk of my rental car, I was exhausted and I collapsed behind the wheel. As I went to start the car, I noticed that I had something attached to my steering wheel.

"Phil!" I yelled, practically jumping out of the car to get away from it.

I looked around, but Phil was gone. He already fled the scene of the crime.

The dildo was strapped to my steering wheel. It stretched from the nine o'clock to three o'clock position. I cut it off the steering wheel and put it in a random helmet in one of the equipment bags.

The dildo, which came to be called the Staff of Power, disappeared. We forgot about it for a few months until back in Virginia Beach after we finished some gas-mask training.

Since DEVGRU is tasked with hunting down weapons of mass destruction, we often trained in the kill house in full chemical suits. The gas masks took a while to get used to, and we had to be comfortable operating in the suits and masks for long periods.

It was the end of the day, and we all came up to the team room after to get a beer. I walked in and headed over to the refrigerator. Popping the cap and taking a long pull, I turned back and saw some of the guys huddled around the foot of the conference table.

"Holy shit," I heard one of them say.

"No way, that isn't it, is it?" another one said.

I walked over to the crowd and saw a Polaroid picture taped to a blank sheet of paper. The Staff of Power was coiled in someone's gas mask. As soon as I saw the picture, my stomach flipped. I had no idea where the Staff had been before Phil snagged it, and now it could have been in my gas mask. The same mask I spent hours in that day. I tried to see if the mask in question was mine, but the picture was shot so tightly it was impossible to tell. In that minute, the Staff of Power was in everybody's mask, and no one was going to take a chance.

I followed the crowd down to supply and traded in my mask for a new one. Again, the Staff of Power was missing in action for a few months.

There was always food in the kitchen, and guys used to bring in massive jugs of pretzels and other snacks from Costco. One day a bin of animal crackers appeared in the team room. Handful by handful, the crackers started to disappear. You'd see guys eating the crackers as they walked from the kitchen to their cages or out to the ranges.

Soon enough, about halfway through the jug we found

another Polaroid picture. This time, the Staff of Power was jammed into the middle of the bin with animal crackers piled up around the shaft.

To this day, I still can't eat animal crackers.

I have no idea if Phil was the culprit. I know he was the one who found it, but to date the Staff of Power is unaccounted for.

CHAPTER 6

Maersk Alabama

The only thing Phil loved more than a good prank was parachuting. As my team leader, Phil had a passion that drove our team to air operations, in particular High Altitude, High Opening (HAHO) jumps. The technique offered the best and most stealthy way to infiltrate a target. During a HAHO jump, you exit the aircraft, open your parachute a few seconds later, and fly your canopy to the landing zone.

I got my free-fall qualification at Team Five, but it wasn't until I got to DEVGRU that I truly mastered the art of jumping.

Let me be clear, at first jumping out of an airplane scared me.

There is something unnatural about walking to the edge of the ramp and jumping out. Not only did it scare me, I hated it at first. I was the guy sucking down oxygen on the ride up. After every jump, when I was back on the ground, I loved it. But the next morning, I'd sweat it all over again. By forcing myself to do it over and over, eventually it became easier. Just like in BUD/S, quitting wasn't an option and jumping was a big part of our job, so it was something I learned to love.

While I was with Delta on my 2005 deployment to Iraq, Phil successfully led a HAHO jump in Afghanistan. We always trained for this type of mission but I never thought I'd do one for real. Since I'd joined the command, I rotated between Iraq and Afghanistan, deployment after deployment. Things had fallen into a pattern of deployments, training, and standby. There were so many missions they started to blur together. We were rapidly gaining combat experience with each deployment. The command as a whole continually refined its tactics and had become even more combat effective.

In 2009, we finally got something different.

I was on personal leave, waiting for a commercial flight back to Virginia Beach, when I saw the breaking news bulletin flash across the TV screen in the airport. The *Maersk Alabama*, a cargo ship with seventeen thousand metric tons of cargo, was headed for Mombasa, Kenya, when Somali pirates attacked it in transit near the Horn of Africa. It was Wednesday, April 8, 2009. The pirates captured the *Maersk Alabama*'s captain, Richard Phillips, and fled with the captain in one of the ship's eighteen-foot covered lifeboats. They had nine days of food rations. The USS *Bainbridge*, a destroyer, was shadowing the lifeboat, which was motoring about thirty miles off the Somali coast. Four pirates were on board armed with AK-47s.

Sitting in the airport, I wondered if we were going to get the call. Getting personal time off was a huge feat since my squadron was on standby and could be called to deploy anywhere in the world with an hour's notice.

Watching the TV at the airport, I could see the orange lifeboat bobbing in the surf. Nearby was the gray-hulled USS *Bainbridge*. I tried to stand close so I could hear the report over the noise of the airport. Nothing was going on when I'd left Virginia Beach a few days earlier, but now I had a feeling we'd be getting a call. As footage of the lifeboat popped up on-screen again, my phone buzzed in my pocket. It was Phil.

"You watching the news?" he said.

"Yeah. Just saw it," I said.

"Where you at?"

At this point, I was the most senior member of my team besides my team leader.

"I am at the airport," I said. "I am literally waiting for my flight."

"OK, good," Phil said. "Get back as soon as you can."

Instantly, I could feel my mind racing. The plane couldn't fly fast enough. This mission was a once-in-a-lifetime chance. I didn't want to miss it.

Boarding a plane is frustrating enough when you're not in

a rush. I watched as folks meandered to their seats or fussed with the overhead bins. I pleaded with them in my head to hurry. The sooner we took off, the faster I could get back to work. Plus, I knew once I was airborne I'd be in a communications blackout. There was no way to contact me if they got the word to go. For all I knew, as the flight attendant sealed the doors to my plane, I was getting the recall notice telling me I had one hour to get to the command, and by the time we landed the team would be gone.

Putting my headphones in, I tried to zone out but I couldn't. Five steps from the gate after we landed in Virginia I was on the phone.

"Hey, what's up?" I said when Phil picked up.

It was well after eight at night, since I'd come from the West Coast.

"Still here," he said. "Come into work tomorrow early and I will get you up to speed. Planning is underway. But we're waiting for D.C. to make a decision."

The next morning, I was at work early. Phil met me in the squadron room. We sat down at the conference room table.

"We've got one hostage," Phil said. "Four pirates. They want two million dollars for him."

"Nothing like knowing exactly what you're worth," I said.

"I'd ask for more," Phil said. "A couple of million seems a bit light, unless you ask my ex-wife."

"Where are they going?" I asked.

"They want to link up with their buddies and try and get Phillips to a camp or a mother ship," Phil said. "So, we've got to be ready to do a ship takedown or go over the beach and take out one of the camps."

We'd spent years preparing for either mission.

"We've already got a handful of guys on the *Bainbridge*," Phil said. "They were working in Africa and jumped in last night. Negotiations broke down Thursday."

"How long do we have before they make shore?" I asked.

"They don't want to make landfall where they are now because of some tribal issues," Phil said. "Their tribe is a little farther south so they can't make landfall for another two days, so hopefully we have a timeline to work against."

I asked about the recall.

"No recall, but it's being discussed," Phil said.

"Why haven't we heard anything yet?" I said. "It doesn't make any sense that it takes this long to make a decision."

"Dude, it's Washington," he said. "Does anything make sense?"

A day later, we finally got a page recalling us. Most of us were already at the command. Our gear was packed and ready.

About twenty hours later, the ramp of the C-17 cracked open and sunlight spilled into the cabin.

I could feel the breeze on my face as I shielded my eyes from the bright East African sun. Minutes later, I saw the small parachute attached to a massive gray high-speed assault craft (HSAC) snap open and start to drag the boat out of the back of the plane. The boats were loaded with all the gear we needed. The plan was to drop them and the crews first, followed by the assault teams.

CLICK. CLICK. CLICK.

I could hear the boat on the metal rollers as it started toward the door, picking up speed before disappearing off the ramp. Moments later, a second parachute opened and the gray blur of the second boat flew past as it shot out, followed by the boat crews.

"Yeah," I yelled as I watched the boats go. Others around me cheered as the boat crews disappeared off the ramp.

My heart was beating faster, more from excitement than anything else, as I waited for the thumbs-up from my teammates on the ramp. They were watching to make sure the chutes on the boats opened.

We were jumping over the horizon from the USS *Bainbridge* so the pirates couldn't see us. The USS *Boxer*, an amphibious assault ship used to carry Marines into battle, was going to rendezvous with us and we'd stage off of her deck.

In the water below, the boat crews landed near the HSACs and started clearing off the parachutes. We had thirty minutes to wait before we jumped, which seemed like much longer.

I was sitting near the front of the plane on one of the bench seats. On top of me was one of my squadron's communications specialists. He was wearing a tandem passenger harness strapped to the front of me. Hours before, he'd learned that not only was he going to Africa to help us with a hostage situation but he was also going to jump into the Indian Ocean to do it.

In order to get all needed personnel down to the USS *Boxer*, we had to jump three tandem passengers, including the communications specialists. These three non-SEALs were essential support personnel. During the flight over, I had a chance to sit down with the communications tech and brief him.

"You're mine," I said to him. "You ready for this?"

He was thin with a short haircut and a bookish demeanor. He looked a little nervous when I started to go over the jump and what to expect.

"You ever jumped before?" I asked.

"No," he said.

When we got the six-minute call, everyone stood up to do our last-minute checks. I noticed the communications specialist looked pale. He hadn't said a word since the door opened the first time. At least my first jump was over Arizona. His was a real-world jump into the Indian Ocean.

"We're going to be fine," I said.

He didn't look convinced.

The ramp opened again. There were about forty jumpers on the plane, and we lined up on the ramp.

"Stand by," the jumpmaster yelled, giving us the signal that we had less than thirty seconds before the jump.

I could feel the communications specialist's leg start to shake. It was practically vibrating as we got closer to the ramp.

"Hey, buddy, just relax," I said.

All I needed him to do was remember everything I had told him.

"Green light, GO!"

The jumpmaster pointed off the ramp.

Up ahead, everyone started waddling to the ramp and diving off one by one. As we got closer to the ramp, I could see the sky and water meet at the horizon. I reached up and tapped my passenger on the shoulder twice and screamed over the wind into his ear.

"HANG!"

That was the signal to get into position. I wanted his toes hanging over the edge of the ramp so when we dove out I didn't rake his shins on the ramp.

He froze. I could feel his feet try and dig into the ramp. I tapped him again and yelled.

"HANG!"

Again, he didn't move.

We didn't have time to wait. I pushed him forward and we dove off the ramp.

The drogue chute popped off my back. The small parachute helped stabilize us and controlled our speed during free fall. Just like during hundreds of other jumps, I went through my checks and pulled the handle and opened the main canopy.

Suddenly, all the airplane noise bled away and everything was perfectly quiet. The only sound was the chute snapping in the wind.

Looking around, it was beautiful. The fresh air was a welcome relief from the C-17 cabin. The sky and water were the same crystal blue and only a few wispy clouds were high above us. Scanning below me, I could see a maelstrom of parachutes all circling the four gray boats bobbing on the ocean below.

It looked like a World War II dogfight as my teammates swooped around in circles avoiding one another and coming to rest in the ocean.

The water was calm, with very small waves. Not far off I could see the flat deck of the USS *Boxer* waiting for us. As we came in, I flared out the parachute and splashed down into the bathtub-temperature water. Unhooking the communications specialist, I started to work my way out of the parachute harness.

We weren't more than twenty yards from the boat. Sliding my flippers off my ankles, where I'd taped them for the jump, I started to swim over to the communications specialist. Behind me, the chute started to slip below the surface as the reserve parachute filled with water, dragging it to the bottom. I swam up to the communications specialist as he paddled, in a life jacket, toward the ladder hanging off the boat.

"How was it, dude?" I said.

"That was crazy," he said.

It was the first time I saw him smile since the ramp opened.

Climbing aboard the HSAC, I found a place near the front while we waited to get a head count. Since the boats were only built for twelve people, it got crowded quickly. I climbed to the bow and let my feet dangle in the water. I let the current push my fins around.

"Hey man, did you see any sharks?" one teammate said to me as he climbed into the bow area.

"No," I said. I knew the waters around here were infested, but I hadn't noticed anything coming in.

"Dude, as I was coming in I saw this massive shadow below," he said.

I slid my fins closer to the boat.

During our flight over, Phillips tried to escape, ratcheting up tensions. He made it into the water before being fished out at gunpoint. The pirates bound the captain's hands and threw a phone and American two-way radio into the ocean, thinking the captain was somehow taking orders from the ship.

By now, the lifeboat was out of fuel and was adrift. Commander Frank Castellano, captain of the USS *Bainbridge*, persuaded the pirates to be towed by the destroyer, and to allow the ship's rigid-hulled inflatable boat to deliver food and water. During one of the supply runs, the fourth pirate, Abduhl Wal-i-Musi, asked for medical attention for a cut hand. He was transferred to the *Bainbridge* for treatment. He'd been injured when Phillips attempted to escape.

After setting up on the USS *Boxer* on Saturday, we sent a small team over to the USS *Bainbridge*. The rest of the squadron was told to hold tight. In the event that the lifeboat made landfall, we would be forced to attempt a rescue mission on shore.

The team that went over to the *Bainbridge* was made up of an assault team, multiple snipers, and a small command element. The SEALs set up an overwatch position on the fantail of the *Bainbridge*. Snipers started a rotating watch as negotiations continued. We waited patiently for the situation to develop.

On Sunday, we suddenly got word that Phillips was now on board the USS *Bainbridge* and safe. Soon all the guys were back and I ran into my friend Gary. He was in the class ahead of me during BUD/S. Gary came to Green Team a few years after me. He started his SEAL career driving mini subs. It was funny to think of him folding his six-foot-four-inch frame into the sub. He was awarded a Silver Star on the last deployment. He literally stitched up five guys trying to flank his element during a mission in Kandahar. Gary went over to the *Bainbridge* and was in charge of interrogating the captured pirate Wal-i-Musi.

We shook hands.

"Dude, holy shit, give me some scoop." I said.

"We caught the last one when he popped his head up and smoke checked all three," Gary said.

Gary told me he was tasked with talking to the injured pirate, Musi. Gary hoped the pirate could persuade his comrades to surrender. Gary started killing Musi with kindness when he got to the *Bainbridge*.

"Hey, man, want some ice cream?" he said. "How about a cold Coke?"

Musi and Gary struck up a quick friendship over food and comfort. Gary kept Musi out in the open so the other pirates could see him drinking Cokes and eating ice cream. Since the pirates still on the lifeboat had to yell back and forth to negotiate.

"I can't hear," Gary told Musi. "Tell them to pull the rope in."

Musi agreed and the line got shorter and shorter, the lifeboat inching closer to the *Bainbridge*. The seas were getting rough and with no engine the lifeboat was getting tossed around. As it got dark, Gary and his teammates pulled the lifeboat even closer. It was pitch-black and there was no way the pirates could tell they were being pulled closer to the USS *Bainbridge*. On the fantail, Gary and his teammates scanned the lifeboat. Infrared lasers that can be seen only through night vision goggles danced over the skin of the boat.

One of the pirates always sat on top of the covered area keeping watch; engaging him would be simple. They could also see one pirate through the window steering the boat, another relatively easy target. But the third pirate was always hidden, and they needed to take out all three at the same time. The only way to take the shots and ensure Phillips's safety was to get the third pirate to expose himself. Finally, after hours of waiting, on Sunday night the third pirate's head and shoulders emerged from the rear hatch of the lifeboat. That was all the snipers needed. The orders stated, only act if Phillips's life was in imminent danger. With tensions already high, and fearing for Phillips's safety, my teammates opened fire. In seconds, all three pirates crumbled under the barrage.

After the last of the sniper shots rang out, the team on the fantail heard one unmistakable crack from a pirate's AK-47. The single shot echoed over the water, and my teammates were immediately deflated. The stakes were high. Washington was getting frequent updates, and they were watching drone feeds of the lifeboat. The commanding officer of DEVGRU and our squadron commander were both on the USS *Boxer*.

Fearing the worst and not knowing if Phillips was dead or wounded, two snipers near the towline jumped up and started to slither down the rope to the boat. There was no time to waste. Balancing on top of the towline, which bobbed inches above the dark waves, they reached the boat in minutes. Armed with only pistols, they boarded the lifeboat and swung inside the enclosure. There was a single opening into the raft, making them an easy target for even a wounded pirate.

Entering the life raft, they quickly and methodically re-engaged each pirate, making sure there was no more threat. They found Phillips tied up in the corner, unhurt. The USS *Bainbridge*'s rigid-hull inflatable boat carrying a handful of SEALs was shadowing the lifeboat. When they heard the shots, the boat raced in and the SEALs pulled Phillips off the lifeboat.

Back on the *Bainbridge*, before the last shot rang out, Gary grabbed Musi and slammed him onto the deck.

"You're going to jail," he said. "Your buddies are dead. You're useless to me now."

With his hands cuffed and a hood pulled over his head, Musi was led away.

Gary met Phillips at the fantail. The captain was confused and disoriented as he climbed on board the *Bainbridge*.

"Why did you guys have to do that?" Phillips said.

He was suffering from a minor case of Stockholm syndrome and in the shock of the shootings, he didn't understand what had just happened and why.

Phillips underwent a medical exam and was found to be in relatively good condition. It didn't take long before the Stockholm syndrome wore off. He was thankful for what my teammates had done. He called his family and was flown to the USS *Boxer* before heading home to Vermont.

The rest of us spent a few more days on the USS *Boxer*, waiting for follow-on orders before moving ashore and then flying home. It felt good to finally save a life instead of just taking guys out. It was cool to do something outside of Iraq and Afghanistan. I was happy to do something different. But the downside was we got a glimpse of the Washington machine and just how slow the decision-making could be. We were ready to launch on this days before we actually got the call. But the Captain Phillips mission renewed our capabilities and put us on Washington's radar for other high-profile missions.

CHAPTER 7

The Long War

My legs ached and my lungs burned as I raced up the mountain.

It was summer 2009 and we were about eight thousand feet up in the central Afghan mountains two hours south of Kabul. After the Phillips rescue, we returned home, trained for several months, and then deployed on schedule to Afghanistan.

I could see the infrared laser from the aerial drone tracking the movement of eight fighters who ran out of the target compound when we arrived. Our team tore off after them as soon as the helicopter's ramp hit the ground.

"Alpha Team has visual on squirters," was all I heard Phil say over the radio.

The fighters were headed for a ridgeline three hundred meters north of the compound. We were trying to cut them off while the rest of the troop took down the compound. As we closed on their position, I looked back to see Phil and the rest of the team close behind. It was our first mission on this deployment, and we were still getting used to the altitude.

Seeing the rest of the team moving into position, I snapped back around and shouldered my rifle. The enemy fighters were setting up a fighting position roughly one hundred and fifty yards away. I could barely keep my laser steady after the five-hundred-meter run in all of my gear, but I managed to lock on to the fighter with a PKM machine gun. Squeezing off multiple rounds, I watched him fall. By then, my teammates arrived and opened fire, dropping two more fighters before the rest disappeared over the ridgeline and out of sight.

Leaving their dead, the remaining fighters raced down the backside of the ridge.

"We have five hotspots moving to the north toward several compounds," I heard the drone pilot say in my radio. I could see the laser from the drone moving down the backside of the hill.

Phil gave the team a nod, and we were off on another dead sprint to close the distance.

As we crested the top of the ridgeline, we slowed down, careful not to rush into a hasty ambush. I saw three bodies lying there, one with the machine gun and one with an RPG. We were lucky to take out their two biggest guns in the first seconds of the fight.

The dead fighters were dressed in baggy shirts and pants and black Cheetahs, high-top Puma-like sneakers worn by Taliban fighters. It was a running joke in the squadron that if you wore black Cheetahs in Afghanistan, you were automatically suspect. I've never seen anyone but Taliban fighters in those sneakers.

From the ridgeline, we could see the surviving fighters tearing down the backside of the hill. Phil snatched the RPG lying next to one of the dead fighters and fired it at the group as they ran off. The rocket landed nearby, and the shrapnel peppered the fighters as they ran.

Dropping the launcher, he turned to me. Over the radio, we were getting calls about close air support, or CAS. An AC-130 gunship was circling above us.

"CAS IS COMING ON STATION," Phil literally screamed at me from two feet away.

The RPG had knocked out his hearing.

"I can hear you," I said. "Stop screaming."

"WHAT?" Phil said.

For the rest of the night, I could hear Phil before I saw him. Every word out of his mouth came in a scream.

We watched from the ridgeline as the AC-130's 20mm cannon pounded the fighters. Sending the combat assault dog, which Phil had nicknamed the "hair missile," ahead, we spent the rest of the night chasing down the remaining fighters. All of them were either mortally wounded or dead.

Phil and another assaulter chased a fighter into one of the compounds, while the rest of us started to clear a field of waist-deep grass. The AC-130 was reporting more hotspots. We launched the hair missile and he locked on to the scent of a fighter about fifty feet to my right. I could hear the fighter start screaming as the dog attacked.

Calling the dog off, the assaulters threw hand grenades into the ditch where the fighter waited to ambush us. As they moved up to clear the ditch, I started to move forward.

Even under my night vision goggles, it was difficult to see. The grass was thick and hard to walk through. Behind me, I could hear intermittent gunfire as Phil and another assaulter were in a firefight with a barricaded shooter in one of the compounds. My gun was up and I tried to use my laser to illuminate a path through the grass. I could see burnt patches ahead of me where 20mm shells had hit.

Every step was measured.

I saw a dark shadow at my feet, underneath my night vision goggles. I lifted my foot to step on it, assuming it was a log or a branch, when I heard a man gasp. I jumped back and opened fire. It scared the shit out of me.

Taking a second to confirm I didn't actually shit myself, I got my nerves under control. I moved up to search the body. He must have been dead before I got there. The weight of my foot on his chest forced the air out of his lungs. The body was singed from the 20mm rounds. After a quick search, I found an AK-47 and a chest rack.

Back in Jalalabad, we posed for some pictures after the mission. Phil, wearing a black Under Armour skullcap, had the RPG draped over his shoulder. The picture would be a reminder of the time he cut down the enemy with their own RPG and blew out his hearing.

It was a good night's work and a great start to a lively deployment. That night, we killed more than ten fighters and suffered no casualties. As usual, it was a combination of skill and luck. Without a doubt, the shooter in the ditch would have ambushed us, which proved the value of the combat assault dog.

Since arriving at the unit, my life had been a series of highs from great operations and then days of lows waiting for the next mission. If we weren't deployed, we were training to deploy. We'd alternate deployments between Iraq and Afghanistan. The pace was nonstop. It didn't matter if you were single or married with kids. Our whole world was focused on our work. It was our number one priority.

It isn't smart for me to get too much into families for security reasons, but it is also dishonest to make you think we didn't have them. We had wives, kids, girlfriends, ex-wives, and parents and siblings all vying for our time. We tried to be good fathers and spouses, but after years of fighting the war it was hard to be present even when we were at home.

We lived with one eye on the news, waiting for the next Captain Phillips story. When we trained, we did it in a way that was as accurate as possible. We were too busy doing our normal deployment, training, and keeping the wheels on the bus at home to think of much else.

For the most part, our families understood the lifestyle. When we're gone eight to ten months out of the year on training or deployment, they always ended up being the last priority.

They wanted us home.

They wanted us safe.

They knew very little of what was really going on in our lives. They never experienced the satisfaction of knowing that every IED maker or al Qaeda fighter we killed made the world a little safer, or at least made life easier for the soldiers patrolling along the roads in Afghanistan. They might understand it in theory, but they were always left at home to worry.

The families waited for the men in dress uniforms to arrive at their door and deliver the news that we weren't coming home. The SEAL community has lost a lot of great guys, and DEVGRU alone has lost more than its share. Those sacrifices have not been for nothing. The lessons we learned and the heroic actions of our brothers were not going to be in vain. We knew the risks on deployments and in training. We knew how to live with them, and we understood that we had to sacrifice to do this job. Our families, like my father who hadn't wanted this lifestyle for me, didn't always understand.

Just before my high school graduation in Alaska, I told my parents my plan to enlist. My parents weren't pleased. My mother didn't let me play with G.I. Joe or other military toys when I was younger because they were too violent. I still joke with my mother that had she let me play with action figures and get it out of my system I might not have joined the military.

Before graduation, I sat in the kitchen and talked on the phone with recruiters. At first, I think my parents thought it was a phase. But soon they realized how serious I was about joining the Navy.

My father sat me down to talk about my plans and about college.

"I just don't want you in the military," he finally said.

He wasn't a pacifist by any means, but he'd grown up during Vietnam and knew how war impacted people. A lot of his friends had been drafted and hadn't come back. He didn't want his son to ever go to war. But I didn't hear the concern in his voice or the nervousness about his only son putting himself in harm's way. I just heard him tell me what I couldn't do.

"I'm doing it," I said. "This is what I want."

My father never raised his voice. Instead, he reasoned with me.

"Hear me out," he said. "If you ever listen to anything I say, will you take one piece of advice from me? Try one year of college. If you don't like it, you don't have to go back."

My dad knew that I hadn't seen much of the world growing up in a small village in Alaska. They were betting if they could talk me into going to school, I'd be exposed to so many new things that I wouldn't pursue my dreams of becoming a SEAL.

I was accepted to a small college in southern California.

"OK, Dad," I said. "One year."

One year turned into four, and with my degree I considered joining the Navy as an officer. I made friends with a former SEAL in school who advised me not to join as an officer. He told me I could always become an officer later, but the enlisted route meant more time as an operator and allowed me to stay in the fight. When I enlisted after college, my father had no objections.

Like all of my teammates, I was driven to be a SEAL. And once I finished BUD/S, I was driven to be the best SEAL I could be. I wasn't unique. There was a whole command of guys just like me. But like me, they all struggled with balance. We called it "the speeding train"; it was hard to get on, and it was hard to get off, but once you're there you'd better hang on because you're in for a ride.

We really had two families: the guys at work and then family and loved ones left at home. I came from a tight family in Alaska. I felt the same way about them as I did about my teammates, like Phil, Charlie, and Steve.

For a lot of guys, keeping the balance between work and family life was fleeting. Many of my teammates suffered through bitter divorces. We missed weddings, funerals, and holidays. We couldn't tell the Navy no, but we could tell our families no. And we did, often. It was difficult to get time away. Work was always the number one priority. It took everything out of you and gave back very little.

The funny thing was, even when we were on leave before a deployment, I'd see guys at work. We came in to work on gear, work out, or just take care of last-minute issues before we deployed.

The dirty secret of it all is that everyone, including me, loved it. We wanted to get the call every time, which meant everything else in the world took a backseat.

I was on my eleventh consecutive combat deployment in 2009. I had worked my way up from a new guy to being Phil's number two. From 2001, the only break I had was Green Team, if you call that a break. That was eight years straight of either going on missions or training for them. By now, I was smarter and more mature. As I moved up, new guys came in behind me. The new guys now had more combat experience. They were certainly better than I was when I arrived at Green Team. The command as a whole was better. We were primarily focused on Afghanistan. Even with operations in Iraq winding down, our pace never lagged. We all wanted to work, but all of the senior guys were starting to feel the miles.

Steve had moved up. He was in charge of one of the other teams in our troop. Charlie was an instructor in Green Team.

It was a summer deployment, which meant we were busy. The annual Taliban summer offensive was in full swing. During the winter, the fighting slowed because it was cold and miserable. When an American soldier went missing at the start of the summer, we dropped everything to find him.

Private First Class Bowe Bergdahl disappeared on June 30, 2009. A Taliban group captured him and quickly moved him closer to the border between Pakistan and Afghanistan in hopes of getting him across. Our intelligence analysts tracked every lead after his disappearance, and we launched on several rescue attempts but came up empty. It was a race to get him back before they smuggled him to Pakistan. The fear was that the group that captured him would eventually sell him to other groups like the Haqqani network, a terrorist group allied with the Taliban.

Less than a month after he disappeared, the Taliban released a video showing Bergdahl, dressed in the baby blue long shirt and baggy pants of the region, sitting in front of a white wall. He was lean, with a long neck and a little scruff under his chin. In the video, he looked frightened.

One evening just after the first video appeared, we got word they might have a possible location for him.

"Intelligence says he was likely in this area south of Kabul today," our troop commander said, pointing at a map of central Afghanistan. "We don't have much intel to go off of, but this is a priority."

We were gathered up for a mission brief at the operations center. Steve and his team were there too. The entire troop was slated to go. The plan was to fly to the "Y," which means landing just outside of RPG range and then moving into position. It wasn't as safe as patrolling in, but it wasn't as dangerous as flying to the X. It was the only way we could assault the target and clear it before the sun came up.

It was already midnight, which meant we were running out of darkness. So we had to launch immediately.

"We've got one hundred percent illumination tonight, so it will be bright as fuck out there, fellas," Phil said.

Typically, we try not to operate when the moon is full. Our night vision works even better, but the high illumination means the enemy could see us too, cutting our advantage in half.

Tactical patience is key. We typically liked to wait and develop a target, and then hit it with the odds stacked in our favor. We weren't fighting second graders. The Taliban are good fighters and we already knew the operation had the potential to get squirrelly.

"Hey guys, we are getting our hands forced a little here," the troop commander said. "We need to accept a little more risk because of who we're going after."

A cloud of dust covered me as I ran off the ramp of the CH-47 Chinook helicopter. We landed in an open field, and my team's job was to move west of the target while Steve and his team moved south, creating a loose "L" shape as we moved toward a cluster of compounds where we thought Bergdahl might be held.

The target was an hour-and-a-half helicopter ride from our base in Jalalabad. There was a house on the edge of the landing zone. Steve's team took a few steps off the ramp before fighters started spilling out of it. One of the Taliban fighters had a PKM machine gun. I could hear the automatic weapons fire over the rotor noise as I ran.

Looking over my shoulder back at the helicopters, I saw the tracer rounds, like lasers, cut through the dust cloud and zip past the helicopter. I could just make out Steve's team diving for cover and instantly maneuvering on the enemy.

Under effective machine gun fire, one of Steve's teammates pulled out his pirate gun, a small single-shot grenade launcher. In a one-in-a-million shot, he popped up between machine gun bursts and lobbed a grenade into the house, which landed perfectly inside the door. I heard a muffled explosion and saw smoke start pouring out of the door. The grenade suppressed the fire immediately, giving Steve and his team vital seconds to close on the house without taking any casualties. Stacking next to the door, they cleared the house and killed the remaining fighters.

"We've got movers to the north and to the east," Phil said over the radio.

With so much moonlight, I could see like it was daylight. If they could make us out with a naked eye from one hundred meters away, using our night vision we could see them at three hundred meters.

The field in front of us was perfectly flat, and I could see fighters with weapons slung on their backs, racing away from the helicopters. A road ran from north to south across the field, past the compounds and out of the valley. I could just make out two guys on a pair of mopeds racing away. Phil spotted a group of four fighters running west away from the road toward a small house.

"I've got me plus two," Phil said. "We'll take the guys to the west. You take the guys on the bikes."

Steve's team cleared the target compound. There was no sign of Bergdahl, but we figured he had to be somewhere nearby. There were too many fighters here, and they were well armed.

With me were two snipers from our reconnaissance unit, called RECCE, plus the EOD tech. Phil took the dog team and one assaulter.

As we ran across the field, we practically stepped on top of a fighter hiding in the grass. I didn't see him at first; one of the snipers made him out and opened fire. As we moved forward, I noticed he was wearing Cheetahs. Guilty.

Moving forward again, I saw the fighters' mopeds parked just off the road. I picked up two heads popping up over a hay bale, which had to be four to five feet tall at least, and ten or fifteen feet wide.

"I've got a visual on two pax roughly three hundred meters at twelve o'clock," I said.

In military jargon, "pax" are people. The snipers saw them too, and we stopped in the field and took a knee. We needed a quick plan.

"I'm going to set up on the road and see if I can get a shot," one of the snipers said.

He was one of the most experienced snipers at the command. In a previous deployment in Iraq, he had hunted down an Iraqi sniper who was shooting Marines. It took him weeks, but he eventually found the Iraqi sniper holed up in a house. He shot the Iraqi sniper through a missing brick in the wall.

The road was to the left of the hay bale and had a little rise, giving him some high ground.

"I'll take the right flank," the EOD tech said.

"OK," I said. "I'll take the middle and try and get a hand grenade over the top of the hay bale."

I didn't love this plan, but we didn't really have a choice. With our fields of fire and Phil's team to our right flank, we were limited on how we could maneuver to clear around behind the hay bale.

I trusted the snipers to cover me as I moved up. It was about a two-hundred-meter shot—not easy—but with their scopes and night vision it was not difficult either.

We quickly moved to our positions.

"RECCE set."

I was carrying a small, extendable ladder on my back. I dumped it in the grass and marked it with an infrared or "IR" chemical light.

"EOD set."

Transferring my rifle to my left hand, I knelt down and took a grenade from my pouch. I slid the pin out and held it in my right hand. I took a deep breath and started to sprint toward the hay bale. I could hear only my breathing and the wind whipping by as I tried to close the distance before the fighters peeked over the top again. About halfway to the hay bale, I heard an AK-47 open fire off my right flank. Phil and his crew must have tracked down the enemy fighters.

The sprint didn't take more than a few seconds, but in my mind everything slowed like a television replay. I was less than one hundred feet from the hay bale when a head popped up.

I was in the open with no cover. I couldn't freeze. I had to

An Afghan military gun truck sits in the mountain pass between Bagram and Kunduz. Due to the severe weather conditions, winter deployments tend to be less active than summer deployments.

A view from our base in central Afghanistan. During my deployments in Afghanistan, the natural beauty of the country often struck me.

My primary weapons: a Heckler & Koch MP7 with suppressor (top); a highly modified M79 40mm grenade launcher, a.k.a. the "pirate gun" (middle); and a Heckler & Koch 416 assault rifle with a ten-inch barrel and suppressor (bottom).

My assault kit organized during an Afghanistan deployment. Visible are my pistols, assault rifles, helmet with NVGs, and my sixty-pound vest including ballistic plates.

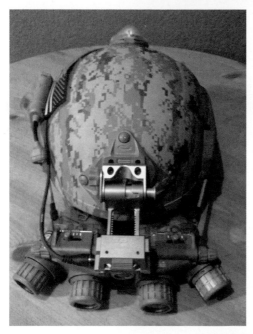

A ballistic helmet outfitted with the latest generation of night-vision goggles, helmet-mounted flashlight, and IR strobe. The four tubes on these NVGs allow better peripheral vision than the standard two-tube goggles. The IR strobe is vital when dealing with helicopters and other aerial assets.

The open ramp of our C-17 moments before we jumped into the Indian Ocean on the Captain Phillips rescue.

HAHO training over the Grand Canyon.

Members of DEVGRU coming in to land during HAHO training.

A CH-47 helicopter, a.k.a. the "flying school bus."

The view out the back of a CH-47. The bags contain fast-ropes.

A CH-47 helicopter like the one we used on the Kunar mission.

MH-6 Little Birds like the ones flown by the Night Stalkers during assaults in Iraq.

Walking into the Iraqi desert for exfil after a long night of work.

get to the hay bale. I didn't have the best arm, so I knew I couldn't clear the hay bale with a throw from this distance. I had to keep closing. A split second later, several rounds from the snipers hit the fighter in the chest, sending him tumbling back like a rag doll.

One of the rounds ignited the propellant on an RPG rocket strapped to the fighter's back. As he tumbled back behind the hay bale, I saw sparks and fire shoot out of his backpack. He looked like a giant sparkler.

Sliding to a stop at the base of the hay bale, I tossed the grenade over the top and rolled away. I heard the crack of the explosion and turned to run.

Under the cover of the sniper, I linked up with the EOD tech and the other sniper in the field. We maneuvered back to the hay bale while the second sniper covered us. Coming around the left side with our guns at the ready, we found one fighter on his back, the RPG still burning underneath him. There was no sign of the other fighter.

As we began the search for the missing fighter, a message crackled across the radio.

"We've got a wounded eagle, we've got a wounded eagle request immediate medevac."

One of the snipers with me was a medic and immediately started moving toward Phil's team. We still hadn't found the missing enemy fighter, so I pushed the thought of who might be wounded out of my mind and three of us continued to search.

I helped the EOD tech gather up the fighters' guns and

mopeds. The fighters had morphine kits and grenades. They were professionals, not some farmers who picked up AK-47s when the crops weren't in season.

We never found Bergdahl on that deployment, and as of the summer of 2012 he was still a prisoner. But in my gut, I think he was there at some point. We probably missed him by a few hours, or maybe in the fight they were able to escape.

After things quieted down, the EOD tech set charges to blow the enemy's equipment.

"I'm ready," the EOD tech said.

We moved to a safe distance, and he set off the charge, blowing the gear and the fighter's body to shreds. The charge gashed the hay bale, setting some of it on fire and leaving a black scorch mark on the rest.

We never found the other fighter's body, but when we went back to make sure the gear was destroyed, we found three human hands. We guessed the fighter probably crawled into the hay bale and died.

Before long, I heard the familiar sound of an inbound CH-47 Chinook. It set down just long enough to hustle the patient on board before it was back in flight and moving fast toward the trauma hospital in Bagram, a massive airfield north of Kabul.

"Alpha 2, this is Alpha 1," Phil said over the radio. I was Alpha 2. Phil was Alpha 1. It was the first time I'd heard from Phil since we split off to chase the squirters.

"Hey, man, take care of the guys for me," Phil said.

The wounded eagle was Phil. He was sitting on the deck

of the helicopter with his pant leg cut open. Blood soaked the deck and his uniform. He was feeling no pain thanks to a heavy dose of morphine.

I found out later his team had been closing the distance on two heavily armed fighters. They sent the combat assault dog ahead. The fighters saw the dog and opened fire. Phil was hit and the dog was killed. The bullet tore open Phil's lower leg. He almost bled out and died, but quick work by our two medics not only saved the leg but also his life.

"Hey, you got it, brother," I said. "Take care."

Walking back to the landing zone to regroup with the troop, the jokes already started.

"Good job taking out Phil so you can be in charge," said one of my teammates. "We saw you shoot him in the leg and run over and grab his call-sign patch."

Phil wasn't even at the hospital yet, and the shit-talking had already begun.

CHAPTER 8

Goat Trails

I had to take a leak.

Since boarding the helicopter thirty minutes before in Jalalabad for the ride to a combat outpost in Afghanistan's mountainous Kunar Province, the pressure had been building. It was standard procedure for everybody to take a leak before you left. But it was such a short ride, I'd decided to hold it until we got there.

It was two months after Phil got shot. He was home recovering. We had about three weeks left on our deployment. I had been a team leader ever since Phil was medevaced. We were heading to a remote forward operating base or FOB in one of the most volatile regions of eastern Afghanistan. The

FOB was going to be a staging area for an operation we were going to conduct high in the mountains.

I could feel the CH-47 Chinook helicopter come to a hover and start to descend. A few seconds after the tires hit, the ramp came down and I dashed off the bird, walking under the massive rear engine headed for a ditch about twenty yards from the landing zone. We landed about fifty meters outside the perimeter of the small firebase, so I felt pretty safe standing out in the open.

I was joined by a few of my teammates who also sought relief. It was pitch-black and no illumination. The mountains towering above me blocked any chance for light. Over my shoulder, the helicopter's blades beat the ground, creating a dust cloud. The roar of the CH-47's engines was deafening.

Standing at the lip of the ditch, I admired the beauty of the steep mountains. Through the green glow of my night vision goggles, it actually appeared quite peaceful. Then my eyes caught the glow of something streaking across the sky. For a split second, I thought I was looking at a shooting star until I realized it was heading right for me.

WHOOM!

A rocket-propelled grenade slammed ten feet off the tail ramp of the helicopter, showering my teammates with shrapnel. Before I could react, I saw tracer rounds and more rockets crash around us. I started to move toward a ditch on the other side of the landing zone. Everybody was stunned. In our minds, we were simply using this base as a jumping-off point for our mission. We didn't expect to make contact until we assaulted the actual compound a few hours later.

118

I could hear the whine of the helicopters' engines change as they took off and flew out of the valley. As the second helicopter lifted off in a hurry, its rotor wash set off one of the trip flares that surrounded the perimeter of the small combat outpost we were planning to stage from. The flares, in theory, were set up to alert the base of an attack, but we were now exposed, illuminated by the flare and in the open. We started to peel back in small teams away from the light as the fighters shifted fire toward the base.

I tried to get my pants buttoned up while in a dead sprint. I could hear the thump of the first outgoing mortars and then the steady hammering of an American .50 caliber machine gun as the soldiers at the base reacted to the attack. Sliding into a ditch, we watched as the American heavy weapons started raking the ridgeline. It looked like a Bloomin' Onion at Outback Steakhouse. Guns stuck up on all sides of the base made of Hesco barriers, large wire frames filled with sand.

Once the flare died out and we had the cover of darkness again, we maneuvered our way back to the main gate and inside the protective wall of the outpost.

When we got inside the gate, our medics started working on the wounded. No one was hurt badly, but shrapnel from the RPGs hit an Army Ranger, our interpreter, an Afghan soldier partnered with us, and our combat assault dog. The helicopters were loitering nearby, and when the fire stopped, they raced back into the valley to pick up the wounded.

Once all the wounded were loaded on the helicopters and safely on their way back to the hospital, the troop chief and team leaders met with the FOB's Army company commander and first sergeant inside the command bunker.

Charlie and the rest of the troop waited in the outpost's weight room. Charlie had volunteered to come over for the last couple of months of the deployment and was running with my team. Since Phil had been wounded and I took over, we were a man short and needed an extra shooter. Charlie had just finished his time as a Green Team instructor.

"Heard you shot Phil to get this job," Charlie said when he got in country. "Is that how you get a team now? Better watch your six."

I had missed the big bully, and it was good to have him back.

Once Phil left, the pranking around the camp stopped. I was confident my room was free from glitter bombs, but the mood was never as light as when Phil was prowling around. Most of all, we missed his experience. Much like a football team, we had the "next man up" mentality. We all knew how to do the job, but it was hard to argue against experience. Phil had a ton of it. The pace of operations made it hard to dwell on the past. But he was missed for sure.

Having Charlie back made up for some of it. Fresh off of instructor duties at Green Team, he was sharp, and on this operation he was going to be vital. His experience and calm demeanor under fire were second to none.

The operations center was small, and maps of the area hung on the wall above furniture made of plywood. Antennas stuck up out of the corner of the squat building. Sandbags made up the walls and roof, protection against RPGs and mortar rounds. A radio sat in one corner, and two young Army specialists or junior enlisted men sat nearby monitoring it.

I stood next to Steve and looked at the map.

"Sorry about the welcome party," the Army captain in charge of the outpost said. "We get it about once a week. You just happened to be at the right place at the right time."

Operating in Kunar was tough. I'd argue it was one of the toughest places to effectively target the enemy in the entire country. It was rare that we made the trip up to the province without getting into a fight. Located in the lower Hindu Kush, the mountains and narrow valleys with steep sides serve as formidable natural obstacles. The province has been a favored spot of insurgent groups for decades. Its impenetrable terrain, cave networks, and border with the semi-autonomous Pakistani North-West Frontier Province provide significant advantages for militant groups.

Known as "Enemy Central" or "Indian Country," between January 2006 and March 2010 more than sixty-five percent of all insurgent incidents in the country occurred in Kunar. Native Taliban forces mingle with foreign al Qaeda fighters, while mujahedeen militias also operate in the region.

On a table at the center of the room was a map of the area. We all huddled around it. The plan was to patrol deep into a valley to the south of the outpost and conduct a kill or capture operation against a group of high-level Taliban who were having a meeting.

We were coming up near the end of deployment, and this

might be our last chance to hit such a juicy target. It had already been a solid deployment, despite Phil getting wounded and one of the dogs being killed. If we played our cards right, we were going to get a little payback.

From our drones overflying the suspected compound, we observed roving patrols. Over the years, Steve and I had gotten pretty good at spotting what we called "nefarious activity."

Drone feeds by themselves don't look like much. On the screen, people look like small ants moving around, but to me and Steve, everything we could see on the feed was adding up. Most compounds don't have roving guards. Combine that with the location in Kunar and intelligence reports about the meeting, and it all added up to nefarious activity.

We knew we were in for a fight.

The plan was for my eight-man team to climb up the ridgeline and parallel the valley until we made our way past the target compound. We would set up a blocking position on the uphill side and contain the fighters in the valley if they tried to escape. They wouldn't expect us on the high ground, since the compounds sat almost at the very top of a valley. The other two teams would patrol up the main road into the valley and try and flush the Taliban fighters out to where my team could ambush them. If the two teams made it all the way to the objective undetected, we would simply make our way down to the compound ourselves and help clear the target from all sides.

Most times, the fighters wouldn't stay and fight when they saw us. Instead, they ran, trying to hide in the tree line or escape into neighboring valleys. To stop them, we set up a team on the high ground and let them wander into our kill zone. We'd cut them down easily before they had a chance to escape.

The infiltration route was about seven kilometers, not far, but only if you didn't account for the elevation change. My team would have to do the majority of the hard climbing that night because the route took us directly up the ridgeline. Knowing we had a very challenging climb ahead, I'd chosen to dump my bulletproof plates and only carry three extra magazines, a hand grenade, my radios, and a med kit. We all tried to go as light as we could. We had a saying: "Light is right."

But when you ditch your bulletproof plates, you have to be willing to suffer the consequences. After our surprise at the landing zone, I was already second-guessing that decision.

As we discussed the plan with the Army captain, I could feel the soldiers' eyes on us. To the clean-cut soldiers, we probably looked like bikers or Vikings.

Most of us had long hair by military standards. None of us had the same uniform on; instead we all had mismatched pants and shirts. We also had fancy, four-tube night vision goggles, thermal scopes, and suppressors on our rifles. We pretty much had all the latest in tactical fashion. Each one of us was a professional who knew exactly what they needed for the job, and it was up to the individual operator to carry what he needed.

"Some of these guys aren't even wearing their plates," said one of the soldiers.

The troop's RECCE team leader showed the captain the goat trail on the map. He was going to navigate the route for my team.

"You guys been up this goat trail?" he asked.

"I've seen it," he said. "It is straight up. What kind of time line are you on?"

"We want to hit and be back before it gets light," the RECCE team leader said.

"There is no way you're going to make it," the Army captain said. "The terrain is impossible, and there is no way you can do it in one cycle of darkness."

Since his unit lived in the valley, we couldn't really argue. It was their backyard. They'd seen the terrain in daylight.

"You guys ever been up there?" the troop chief asked, pointing at the target compounds.

"The furthest we've ever been is here," he said, pointing to a spot not even halfway to where we wanted to go. "It took us six hours, and we made contact and got into a long firefight. We had to move back down out of the valley."

We spent a few more minutes talking about the plan.

The troop chief looked at me, Steve, and the other team leaders.

"What do you guys think?"

This target was too good to pass up. Even with three fewer assaulters and no dog, we still had enough people to clear the objective. The drones watching the target reported no major movements, so we still had the element of surprise. We decided to scrap the plan of my team going up the goat trail and we would all combine into a single patrol taking the road part of the way up the valley, then split off and loop around to the high ground and assault the target from above.

"Let's do it," I said when the troop chief looked to me. Steve also nodded yes.

"You guys are still going?" the captain said.

"Yeah," the troop chief said, finally.

"The attack on the base tonight might be a great cover for action," the Army captain said. "Why don't we send out a patrol with you guys tagging along?"

He'd take about twenty soldiers out and patrol into a nearby village that was just down the valley to the south. We'd follow along at the back of his patrol, before peeling off and sneaking up into the target valley. If people were watching, and they were most likely doing so, we'd hope they would take the bait and follow the main body of the patrol.

"You guys mind if we get some ammo before we go?" the troop chief said.

"Sure. I'll get it."

The captain started to organize a foot patrol, while we went back to brief the guys waiting in the outpost's weight room. It had a few dumbbells, a weight bench or two, and a squat rack wedged into a room no bigger than a small home office. Sandbags protected the room, like the operations center, from mortar attacks.

I replaced the few rounds I fired in my magazine and checked to make sure my team was ready. I could see Walt and Charlie loading their magazines as well. Walt was on

Steve's team, and since arriving out of Green Team he'd become tight with Steve and me.

I'd heard about Walt when he was coming through Green Team. All of the East Coast SEALs seemed to know him, and they kept an eye on him as he worked his way up to the second deck.

No taller than my armpit, he had hair that was already shaggy and a thick brown beard covered his face. He was short, but his cocky swagger compensated for it. He had a healthy dose of little-man syndrome and an inordinate amount of body hair. It seemed like the guy could grow a beard in days.

Walt was supposed to start Green Team a year prior, but got in some trouble and had to delay his plans for an extra year.

Walt and I got along almost immediately. He liked to shoot and loved guns as much as I did. One day on the range, I invited him out to the SHOT show, a shooting, hunting, and outdoors trade show in Las Vegas. Schedule permitting, we would go every year, to meet with vendors and see what kind of new guns and equipment were on the market.

The first day of the trip, I introduced him around to all the vendors. By the second day, my contacts were asking me where Walt was hanging out. At a bar after the show the third night, I found Walt holding court with executives from the National Rifle Association. He had a cigar in his mouth, and he was slapping backs and shaking hands like he was running for office. They all loved him.

Walt was the little guy with the big personality.

The team had a quick huddle and I told them the goat trail idea was scrapped. We were now going to patrol up together.

"We are going to go up the main trail and adjust as we get closer to the target," I said. "Any issues?"

Everybody shook their heads no.

"Nope," Charlie said. "We're good."

It was like playing pickup basketball. We knew what needed to happen and all we needed was the basic plan. If you know how to "shoot, move, and communicate," the rest will fall into place. When operations get too complicated, it tends to slow things down. Every single man standing in the weight room that night had years of experience. Plus, the plan always changed, so it was easiest to keep things simple. We'd done this before and trusted the team.

The patrol snaked out of the gate and started down the paved road toward the village. It was a nice road, probably built with American tax dollars. Less than a kilometer from the gate, we slowly fell back from the main group before taking a right turn and heading up our valley to the west.

We followed the road for two hours. It cut back and forth, with each switchback steeper than the last. Soon we came upon a cluster of cars. I could see a Hilux truck parked on one side of the road and two station wagons with racks on the roof. As I passed, I gazed into the windshields. All of the cars were deserted.

This was as far as they could go.

It was the end of the road. The trail narrowed and got steeper as we patrolled deeper into the valley. With every step

I could feel the altitude and the weight of my equipment trying to slow me down. I was getting tired, and we were only halfway. I hoped all this effort was going to be worth it.

After another hour on the trail, I could see the target compounds and at least two small faint lights on near one of the buildings. Clumps of trees blocked most of my view. The buildings were made of stone and mud and seemed to emerge from the valley walls.

Taking the main road the rest of the way would have been easier, but we knew there were sentries watching the route. We couldn't risk being compromised. The drones continued to report roving patrols in the trees around the main road and compound.

Surprise was key. In most cases the quickest way between two points in Kunar was a goat trail. I'd heard the same line in Alaska growing up. We had no choice but to find another way around. Nobody wanted to be in that valley when the sun came up.

"We're going to move directly up the ridgeline and move our way around," I heard the RECCE team leader say over the radio.

I could almost hear my legs scream, but we all knew it was the right call. The RECCE element was confident that if we shot straight up the ridgeline we'd find the original goat trail that my team was going to use.

From the road, we literally climbed up the mountain searching for the goat trail. Several times I had to tighten the sling on my weapon so I could grab boulders in front as I climbed. If I wasn't pulling myself up the side of the mountain, I was making my own switchbacks as we climbed. No one spoke, but I could hear my teammates grunting as they climbed.

We all saw this as a juicy target. We were willing to do it if we could get the jump on them. Still, with every step, the only thought running through my mind was the target better be worth it.

After a couple of hours of climbing, we finally found the goat trail. My legs were beyond sore now, and it was tough to catch my breath because I was tired. But making it to the trail gave us renewed hope. Without a doubt our RECCE guys were the best in the business and if it weren't for their meticulous planning before the mission there is no way we would have ever been able to pull off this operation successfully.

The goat trail wasn't wider than a foot and straddled the ridgeline. On one side was the cliff face towering over us and the other side was an almost straight drop into the valley. We didn't have time to dwell on how a false step could send you sliding down a near-vertical face. We just spent an hour finding the trail, and dawn wasn't that far away, so time was of the essence.

We had to move.

We finally caught a break when the trail emptied us out into a perfect position slightly above the target compound.

There were three central buildings with a courtyard in the middle, and several additional small structures scattered around the perimeter.

At the foot of the trail were a series of fields cut like stairs into the rock face. It was between seasons and the dirt was dry. Sometimes, the fields were flooded and we'd have to slog through the mud.

Setting up on the tiers, my team took the one that was level with the main target compound.

"Alpha is set," I said over the radio.

Steve's team climbed up one tier above my team and moved to the right flank.

"Charlie is set," Steve said on the radio.

Bravo team climbed down one tier to focus on the southern compounds farther down the hill.

"Bravo is set."

I could feel the adrenaline start to flood my body. I no longer felt tired or sore. Each one of my senses was heightened, and we were all on full alert. If everything went according to plan, we'd catch the enemy by surprise. But if things went bad, we'd be in a gunfight in close quarters.

"Take it," troop chief said over the radio. "Nice and slow."

We started to creep forward. Everyone was quiet, and each step was deliberate. Nothing got our blood pumping more than creeping into an enemy compound, sometimes directly into the rooms of enemy fighters while they were sleeping. This wasn't like other units that had to react to a roadside bomb attack or ambush. This was deliberate and calculated.

Our tactics weren't unique. What made us different was our experience level and knowing when to take violent, decisive action and when to be patient and quiet.

I could feel my heart beating in my chest. Every sound was amplified. We'd take four or five steps and hold. Shouldering my weapon, I focused on my laser as it tracked from window to door to alley searching for any movement. I could see my teammates' lasers doing the same thing.

"Go slow," I thought. "Slow is quiet."

When I got to the first building, I tried the rusty knob of the thick wooden door.

Locked.

Charlie tried the same kind of door on the building right next door. It was also locked.

There was no talking. We didn't have any fancy Navy SEAL hand and arm signals. I just nodded at Charlie, and we started to move around the building to the other side that faced the courtyard.

A small gate led into the courtyard. Walt reached up and cut the cord that held up a sheet that blocked the way.

Moving inside, Steve, Walt, and the rest of the team stacked on multiple doors across the courtyard. I saw a RECCE sniper with a thermal scope on the roof starting to scan for sentries in a dried-up creek bed that ran north to south along the perimeter of the compounds.

My team's point man led us through the same gate, and we approached the front door of our building.

Walt tried the door of his building and it was unlocked.

He slowly pushed it open and saw a man messing with a flashlight. As Walt walked into the room to subdue the man, another man sat up from under some blankets. He was wearing a chest rack, and he had an AK-47 next to him. Walt and another SEAL who entered behind him opened fire, killing both men. Across from Walt's room, Steve opened the door to another room and found a group of women and kids. Leaving one member of his team in the room, Steve led the rest of his team to a door farther down the wall.

A RECCE sniper on the backside of the building Steve's team was clearing was looking for roving sentries. As he scanned the road that ran up the valley, he saw a half dozen Taliban fighters grabbing for their guns through a window. He immediately started firing just as Steve and his team reached the door to the room.

Cracking the door open, Steve could see the fighters scrambling for cover.

"Frag out."

One of Steve's teammates cracked the door just wide enough to toss the grenade into the overwhelmed enemy fighters. I heard the muffle of the explosion as shrapnel peppered the room, killing the fighters.

Just as we reached the door to our building, I could make out the faint sound of a second sniper's suppressed rifle opening fire. A guard was sitting on a rock overlooking the main road. He had an AK-47 slung on his back and an RPG resting next to him.

My point man pushed the front door open and cleared

into the first room. The house had a dirt floor, and sacks of food, clothes, and cans of oil littered the room. Out of the corner of my eye, I watched as the point man opened fire. A fighter, gun in hand, was attempting to jump out a back window and escape. The bullets riddled his back and ass as he tumbled out of the window.

Outside, I heard one of Bravo team's Squad Automatic Weapon gunners, or SAW gunners, go hot.

WHAAAAA!

The machine gun rounds echoed across the valley. It caught me off guard because most of us were using suppressors on our guns to muffle the sound.

"We've got movers coming from the north," I heard over the command net on my radio. We were starting to get reports that fighters were headed toward our position from farther up the valley. This target quickly escalated into three separate firefights, and now we had reports of additional fighters advancing on our position.

The SAW gunner and Bravo team continued to maneuver just down the hill from us. One by one, Bravo team picked off at least five more fighters as they tried to move into fighting positions with RPGs and heavy machine guns. The SAW gunner fired another thirty-round burst as he sprayed the last sentry hiding between boulders in the dried creek bed.

Within minutes, I heard the buzz of an AC-130. On the radio, I could hear the troop commander passing word that the AC-130 was going hot on the movers to the north.

"You've got this," I told my teammate.

I left him and another SEAL in the building while Charlie and I cleared an alley that ran between this building and the one below it. The buildings were on the same tiered steps of land as the fields where we had entered.

The alley was narrow, and it was impossible to see the end because the walls were crowded with junk. I kept getting caught up in low-hanging clothes lines strung up between the two buildings.

With a narrow alley like this, Charlie and I stood on opposite walls. I covered his side of the wall with my laser, and I could see his laser crossing the alley onto the wall in front of me. It was all an angles game.

We crept down the alley, being as quiet as possible. The key was throttle control. We'd go fast when needed, but then go back to being slow and quiet. We were about halfway down the alley when Charlie opened fire.

POP, POP, POP.

I froze. I couldn't see what was in front of me. Charlie let loose a short burst and then started to move forward. I glanced ahead for a split second to see a fighter crumble against the wall three steps ahead of me. As he hit the ground, he dropped a shotgun.

Usually we wore about sixty pounds of gear, including those ballistic plates to protect us from gunfire. Charlie wasn't wearing his plates either.

When we cleared all the way to the end of the alley, we paused to get our bearings.

"If I get shot tonight, no one better tell my mom I didn't wear my plates," I whispered to Charlie.

"Deal," Charlie said. "Same goes for me."

A short time later, we heard the "all clear" call over the radio. The target was secure, but now we had to do sensitive site exploitation, which we called SSE. Basically, we shot pictures of the dead, gathered up any weapons and explosives, and collected thumb drives, computers, and papers.

SSE had evolved over the years. It had become a way to rebut false accusations that the fighters we killed were innocent farmers. We knew that within a few days after the raid, the village elders would be down at the local NATO base accusing us of killing innocent civilians. The kind of innocent civilians who we knew and could now prove carried RPGs and AK-47s. The more SSE we provided, the more proof we had that everyone we shot was guilty.

"We are on a time crunch, fellas, so make it fast," the troop chief said. "We've still got movers to the north."

His voice was drowned out by the sound of the AC-130's 120mm shells landing a few hundred meters up the valley. I checked my watch. It was well past four in the morning. We were running out of darkness, and since the shooting started there was a steady flow of reports coming from the drones alerting us to more fighters coming our way.

With the photos complete, we piled all the weapons and

ammo in the center of the courtyard and set explosive charges on a five-minute delay.

With the RECCE guys in the lead, we quickly and quietly snuck back out the way we'd come. As we raced away from the compound, I heard the explosion and saw a small fireball light up the courtyard as the fighters' weapons and ammunition were destroyed.

The walk back was easier than the walk up. We were high on the adrenaline of what we had just managed to pull off. Several times along the patrol down the hill we had to stop and direct some additional close air support on multiple groups of fighters who were searching for us. We didn't want to be in the valley any longer than we had to, and definitely not at daybreak.

Three hours after clearing the compounds, we were back at the base. The guys slumped down along the walls, exhausted. Everyone was smoked. We sucked down water, power gels, pretty much anything we could get our hands on.

In the operations center, we gave the captain all of our SSE. He could show the elders the evidence when they came down to complain.

"We had seventeen EKIA," the troop chief told the captain, meaning we killed seventeen fighters. "We suspect another seven or eight dead from the AC-130."

The Army captain was stunned as he looked at the pictures on his computer. He and his men rarely got a chance to be on the offensive against the enemy. They were stuck protecting the villages and the roads leading into and out of the valley. It felt really good knowing that we eliminated Taliban fighters harassing the outpost.

On the helicopter back to Jalalabad, I finally had time to reflect on the mission. Sitting near the ramp in the dark, I was amazed that we were able to pull off an operation as dynamic as this one without taking any serious casualties.

From the patrol up the mountain, to the assault, it was a textbook raid incorporating all of the lessons we had learned from previous missions.

Instead of flying in and fast-roping down, we snuck in quietly.

Instead of blowing open all the doors, we crept in and caught the fighters off guard.

Instead of yelling and crashing through the buildings, we used suppressors and kept the noise down when possible.

We used their trails and traveled light and we had beaten them at their own game. All in all, we cleared an objective with more than a dozen well-armed fighters without taking one casualty. The raid was proof that good planning and the use of stealth was a lethal combination.

CHAPTER 9

Something Special in D.C.

I stood in my yard and ran my toes through the grass and looked up into the blue sky.

It was the early spring of 2011. Three weeks before, I had been stumbling over the thick gravel that covers the ground at the American forward operating bases and trying to stay warm through the cold Afghanistan winter. For months, it was nothing but ice, snow, and mud. After constant deployments since September 11, 2001, to one desert country or another, I had grown to appreciate the simple things like a nice green lawn.

I was glad to be home.

The last deployment, for the most part, had been slow.

Winter deployments often were, as fighters moved back into Pakistan to wait for warmer weather. My three weeks of leave were winding down, and my troop would be heading to Mississippi to train. I looked forward to getting back on my gun after the break. It was one of those trips where we could still unwind a bit and just relax.

This would be the first trip in a long time that I wasn't going to be shooting with Steve. His time as a team leader was up. When we returned from the last deployment, he transferred over to Green Team to be an instructor. There was no farewell speech. We got back, put our gear away, and when Steve came back from leave he kicked off as an instructor with the next class.

I was into work early that morning to get in a workout and get my kit together for the trip, when I ran into Steve.

"I need a break," Steve said. "It has been a good run since Green Team, and with all the new rules it has taken all the fun out of the job."

"I hear you," I said. "Got one more rotation as a team leader and then we'll see."

Everyone in the squadron was a combat veteran. The average guy had at least a dozen deployments. Even with the pace and the sacrifices of being away from family, most of us kept coming back for more.

"It's going to be a short break," I said to Steve. "You'll be back soon as a troop chief."

"So we can both learn the art of PowerPoint," Steve said.

Everything in Afghanistan was getting harder. It seemed

with every rotation we had new requirements or restrictions. It took pages of PowerPoint slides to get a mission approved. Lawyers and staff officers pored over the details on each page, making sure our plan was acceptable to the Afghan government.

We noticed there were fewer assaulters on missions and more "straphangers," each of whom performed a very limited duty. We now took conventional Army soldiers with us on operations as observers so they could refute any false accusations.

Policy makers were asking us to ignore all of the lessons we had learned, especially the lessons learned in blood, for political solutions. For years, we had been sneaking into compounds, catching fighters by surprise.

Not anymore.

On the last deployment, we were slapped with a new requirement to call them out. After surrounding a building, an interpreter had to get on a bullhorn and yell for the fighters to come out with their hands raised. It was similar to what police did in the United States. After the fighters came out, we cleared the house. If we found guns, we arrested the fighters, only to see them go free a few months later. Often we recaptured the same guy multiple times during a single deployment.

It felt like we were fighting the war with one hand and filling out paperwork with the other. When we brought back detainees, there was an additional two or three hours of paperwork. The first question to the detainee at the base was always, "Were you abused?" An affirmative answer meant an investigation and more paperwork.

And the enemy had figured out the rules.

Their tactics evolved as fast as ours. On my earlier deployments, they stood and fought. On more recent deployments, they started hiding their weapons, knowing we couldn't shoot them if they weren't armed. The fighters knew the rules of engagement and figured they'd just work their way through the system and be back to their village in a few days.

It was frustrating. We knew what we were sacrificing at home; we were willing to give that up to do the job on our terms. As more rules were applied, it became harder to justify taking the risks to our lives. The job was becoming more about an exit strategy than doing the right thing tactically.

"Good luck," Steve said. "Who knows what we'll see next year?"

I laughed.

"BB guns maybe," I said. "Tasers and rubber bullets?"

The command was small enough that I would still see Steve often, even if we'd miss him on the next rotation to Afghanistan.

I quickly finished getting my kit ready and headed home. It was getting warm in Virginia Beach. Not hot enough to swim in the ocean, but nice enough for short sleeves. I was hustling to get some of the things on my "to do" list done before I left again.

The first one was new mulch for the house.

When I got home, a beat-up old F-150 Ford truck was parked in the driveway. The mulch guy had a tarp laid out with a large mound covering it. He'd load up his wheelbarrow with a pitchfork and deliver a load to one of the flowerbeds and then come back for more. It was a one-man operation.

As he loaded up the wheelbarrow, I walked over to shoot the shit. I'd never met him, but some of my teammates had recommended his work. Spreading mulch was something I should do myself, but with so little personal time, it was easier to pay for it.

"You're in the teams, right?" the mulch guy said between scoops.

"Yeah," I said.

From the look of him, he could have been a SEAL except for his long surfer haircut. He was tall and wiry, and he had tattoos covering both arms. He was wearing a ratty surf T-shirt and worn Carhartt pants.

"Figured, you look the part," the mulch guy said, setting down the wheelbarrow. "I just did Jay's house. You know him?"

"He's my boss," I said. "We're actually headed out to do some shooting next week."

Jay was my squadron commander, but I didn't know him that well. He had taken over the squadron before the last deployment. He didn't go out on missions with us very often, so I never really worked with him. At his rank he was typically found running the Joint Operations Center (JOC) and helping us jump through hoops to get missions approved.

We sometimes called our officers "temps" because they showed up for a few years before moving on to check another box on their career path. They bounced from one job to another, never spending enough time to build the kind of roots the enlisted guys did. We tended to stay with one team for a lot longer. Jay was my fourth commanding officer since being at the squadron.

"I guess he's been pretty busy lately," the mulch guy said.

I was surprised, since we'd been off for the last three weeks. After a deployment, most guys just wanted to hide out. It was normal for someone at Jay's level to have work relating to mission coordination and planning. It just seemed strange that Jay was already so busy since we had been on leave.

"What are you talking about?"

"I did his yard the other day," the mulch guy said between loads. "There is something big going on, and he's been up in D.C."

"What?" I said, confused. "He's supposed to go to Mississippi with us in two days."

At the time, the Arab Spring was raging. Egypt had a new government and protests had sprung up across the Middle East. Civil war had gripped Libya, with rebels calling for NATO support. With hotspots in Syria, not to mention the Horn of Africa and Afghanistan still demanding attention, speculating on what could be spinning up was difficult.

We were briefed weekly on any existing or expected threats worldwide. Our intelligence department went over each region in the world, sometimes with a special emphasis on a certain situation like Libya. The brief usually ended with the latest information and missions in Afghanistan and Iraq. The better informed we were, the more prepared we'd be.

It wasn't uncommon for us to spin up on a mission, conduct rehearsals, only to wait for decision makers in Washington to approve it. Sometimes, like with Captain Phillips, we'd go. But most times, we'd just wait and eventually stand down. Over the years, most of us learned to keep our heads down and focus on the task in front of us, and leave the speculation to others. It saved energy, if nothing else.

I wrote off the mulch guy and was thankful I was a team leader and not an officer. Officers get jerked around ten times more than we do. Either way, I was ready to go have some fun in Mississippi.

This trip to Mississippi wasn't like the time I spent down there in Green Team. I didn't have to worry about picking a bottom five or possibly being sent home for improper CQB. We'd spend half the day at the range and the other half running through the kill house working on our skills and making sure everybody was in sync. We had several new guys in our troop, and we had to make sure they were up to speed.

No one really noticed that Jay and Mike, the squadron's master chief, who is the most senior enlisted SEAL in the unit, weren't there. But the mulch guy's words were stuck in my head. I wondered what was so special in D.C.

We came home on a Thursday. On the way to the airport, I got a text message from Mike.

"Meeting 0800."

Mike was massive like Charlie, with thick arms and a

broad chest. He had been stationed at DEVGRU for as long as I was in the Navy. Like Jay, he didn't go out on many missions.

On the way back, I found out some of the other guys in the squadron received the same message. Charlie called me the night I got back into town.

"You get that text?" he said.

"Yeah. You got any scoop? Heard anything?" I said.

"Nope. I know Walt got it too," Charlie said. "I guess there is some list."

Charlie rattled off a few other names from the list. It wasn't whole teams, but senior guys.

"I can't wait to find out what this is all about," I said. "Sounds suspect."

I got to the command early the next day and changed into my "working" uniform—a Crye Precision tan desert pattern and Salomon low-top running shoes—and dropped my cell phone in my cage.

The meeting was in our secure conference room, which meant no phones. The conference room was on a floor designated as a Sensitive Compartmented Information Facility, or SCIF. Pronounced "skiff," it's an area used to process classified or top secret information. We had special badges that got us through the security doors. The lead-lined walls kept out electronic listening devices.

Inside the conference room, the four flat-screen TVs were dark. There were no pictures or maps on the wall. No one had any idea what to expect. I grabbed a chair at the circular table in the middle of the room. I saw Walt, Charlie, and

Tom, my old instructor from Green Team. He nodded when he saw me.

Tom was Steve's old boss. It was odd not seeing Steve. I had deployed with him for the past eight years. Even if this was a wild goose chase and we got jerked around, it was still strange to spin up on something and not have Steve around. I had a feeling when this turned out to be nothing, he would have the last laugh.

There were almost thirty people in the room, including SEALs, an EOD tech, plus two support guys. With us all crowded inside the room, Mike sat down at the table and started the briefing. Jay, the squadron commander, was absent. Mike seemed a little uncomfortable and didn't provide a lot of detail.

"We are going to do a joint readiness exercise, and we're going down to North Carolina to train," Mike said, passing out a list of gear to pack. "I don't have a lot of information. Just load out your standard assault stuff, and we'll tell you more Monday."

I scanned the list. Nothing on the page—guns, tools, and explosives—was unique or gave away what we'd be doing.

"How long are we going to be gone?" one of my teammates asked.

"Unclear," Mike said. "We leave Monday."

"Do we have berthing or do we need tents?" Charlie asked.

"Berthing and chow will be provided," Mike said.

A couple of other guys asked similar questions, but Mike shut it all down. I started to raise my hand to ask a question.

I was curious how we were going to be organized. Overall there was a lot of experience in the room. They'd drawn us from different teams. On most teams, the new guy usually carries the ladder and the sledgehammer. But looking around the room, we had all senior guys. It looked like some kind of dream team they were putting together.

Before I got my hand up, Tom just looked at me and shook his head. I put my hand down. Tom typically never got too spun up. I was usually a little more vocal. My mind was spinning with questions I wanted answered. Not knowing what we were going to do grated on me, especially with the feeling we were just getting jerked around.

"Let's worry about the load-out," Tom said as we left. "And we'll know more Monday."

We all knew what to do and the gear to pack. I went down to the cages and found one of my guys.

"Hey, brother," I said. "I need to borrow your sledge."

Senior guys grabbing gear like a sledgehammer was rare, which brought even more questions from our teammates.

"You got it," he said. "But why again am I giving up my sledge?"

I didn't have a good answer.

"We're going on an exercise," I said. "They called a bunch of us into a meeting today and we're going down to North Carolina. They're calling it a joint readiness exercise."

I wasn't any more convincing than Mike. My teammate just looked at me with a "what the fuck?" expression on his face.

Back in our squadron's storage area, we started loading

two ISUs—small, square shipping containers—with our gear. It took most of the day, and by quitting time the containers were filled with tools, guns, and explosives.

While we packed, speculation was rampant. Some guys figured we'd be in Libya in a few weeks. Others bet on Syria or even Iran. Charlie, who seemed to be mulling over all of the questions and non-answers, came out with the boldest prediction.

"We're going to get UBL," he said.

Since there is no universal standard for translating Arabic to English, we used the FBI and CIA's spelling of his name, Usama bin Laden, shortening it to UBL.

"How do you figure?" I said.

"Look, when we were asking them about the plan, they said we were going to a place where there is a base with infrastructure," Charlie said. "If we don't need any of these things, we're going back to Iraq or Afghanistan. Somewhere there is an American base. I'd say we're going into Pakistan and we're basing out of Afghanistan."

"No way," Walt said. "But if we are, I've been to Islamabad. It's a shit hole."

Walt and I had already been on one wild-goose chase looking for Bin Laden and his flowing white robes.

It was 2007 and I was on my sixth deployment. This time, I was working with the CIA at Forward Operating Base Chapman in Khost Province.

Khost Province was one of the places where the hijackers who crashed into the World Trade Center and the Pentagon trained. Al Qaeda and Taliban fighters were constantly in the province, slipping easily in and out of neighboring Pakistan.

About midway through the deployment, the whole squadron was called back to Jalalabad from multiple bases throughout the country. One of the CIA's leading sources on Osama bin Laden reported he saw the al Qaeda leader near Tora Bora. It was the same place U.S. forces almost captured him from in 2001.

The Battle of Tora Bora started on December 12, 2001, and lasted five days. It was believed Bin Laden was hiding in a cave complex in the White Mountains, near the Khyber Pass. The cave complex was a historical safe haven for Afghan fighters, and the CIA funded many of the improvements during the 1980s to assist the mujahedeen during the Soviet invasion of Afghanistan.

U.S. and Afghan forces overran the Taliban and al Qaeda positions during the battle but failed to kill or capture Bin Laden. Now the CIA source said he was in Tora Bora.

"They saw a tall man in flowing white robes in Tora Bora," the commander said. "He is back to possibly make his final stand." This was 2007, and 9/11 was six years behind us. Until this point, there was no credible intelligence to his whereabouts. We all wanted to believe it, but the details weren't adding up.

We were going to fly into Tora Bora—which sat on the

Afghanistan-Pakistan border, between Khost and Jalalabad—and raid his suspected location. It sounded great in theory, but the operation was based on a single human source. Single-source intelligence rarely added up. No one could confirm the report, despite dozens of drones flying day and night over Tora Bora. The mission was set to launch a few days after we arrived, but it kept getting delayed.

Every day it was a new excuse.

"We're waiting on B-1 bombers."

"The Rangers aren't in place yet."

"We've got Special Forces heading to the area with their Afghan partner units."

It seemed to all of us that every general in Afghanistan wanted a piece of the mission. Units from every service were involved. The night before the operation was going to launch, they called Walt and me to the operations center.

"Something came up, and you two are going to work with the PakMil," the commander said. "If we get squirters toward the border, we need you guys on the PakMil side to coordinate blocking positions."

"Are we bringing our kit?" I asked.

"Yeah. Bring all your op gear. You may be operating with the Pakis."

Once on the ground, we got word Walt had to stay in Islamabad because the Pakistanis only allowed one of us to move forward. Since I was senior, the mission fell to me. An intelligence officer and a communications tech joined me.

I spent the better part of a week in a small command

center in a U-shaped building made of concrete. I watched feeds from drones doing laps over Tora Bora and monitored the radio.

The night I got into Pakistan, the Air Force started their bombing campaign leading up to the team's air assault into the area. My teammates landed in the mountains high above Tora Bora and started to search the area for Bin Laden and his fighters.

I frequently called the PakMil into the command center to look at the drone feed. Once, the drones spotted what looked like a camp near the border. I could make out tents and several men with guns walking around the area. The men didn't appear to be in uniform, but the PakMil officers said it was a border checkpoint.

It was awkward because I didn't know if I could trust the PakMil officers. Everyone had a different story, and I was stuck in the middle trying to keep it all together. The intelligence officer didn't help, and I felt like a politician trying to keep my hosts and my bosses across the border happy.

After a few days of this balancing act, PakMil shut down my portion after the operation turned out to be a dry hole. There were no squirters, and the next day we headed home. Back in Islamabad, I met up with Walt. He was ready to go back to Afghanistan.

For all the time and effort, we essentially bombed some empty mountains and my teammates went on a weeklong camping trip. There was no sign of any man in flowing white robes. When we finally got back to Afghanistan a week later, "flowing white robes" became an inside joke for a bad mission.

This training exercise down in North Carolina sounded like another bad mission.

But I wouldn't know until Monday. Unfortunately, I needed an extra day in Virginia Beach, which meant the whole team was heading down without me. I hoped my delay wouldn't cost me my slot on the team, just in case it was something big. I stressed to Mike that I could cancel my plans and come down with the team.

"Don't sweat it," Mike said. "Just come down Tuesday morning."

On Monday afternoon, I started texting Walt and Charlie, trying to get some scoop. Both wrote back basically the same message:

"Just hurry up and get down here."

They would have said something if it was lame. The lack of response meant it was legit. I didn't sleep Monday night.

I was up before dawn Tuesday morning. Speeding through a pouring rain, I had to force myself to slow down on the rural roads. I knew something good was on tap, but I also didn't want to slide off the road and wrap my truck around a tree.

The two-hour drive on Tuesday morning felt like eight hours.

Finally rolling up to the gate of the training base around

seven A.M., I met the guard. From the outside, it looked innocent except for the screens hung along the fence to block anyone from looking inside.

Giving him my name, which was on the list, I got my laminated security badges and headed to a building where the team was based. I kept my window down after speaking with the guards. The base was tucked into a pine forest. The morning rain brought out the scent of the trees.

I was three hours early, but I didn't care. I was already a day behind. Not being there almost bothered me more than not knowing. There was no way I was going to wait until late morning to get started. I needed to catch up.

A single-lane cement road led to a gate. Large ten-foot-tall wooden security barriers lined the road, making it impossible to see inside the compound. Pulling through the gate, I started toward the parking lot in front of two 1970s-era two-story concrete buildings.

As I pulled up, I saw two of my buddies walking into one of the buildings. I gave a quick honk and parked in a nearby space. They stopped and waited for me. A light rain was falling, and I hustled over.

"You're early," they said. "We just finished breakfast. What time did you get on the road?"

"Early," I said, skipping right to it. "What do we have?"

I wanted instant gratification.

"You ready?" one said, smiling. "UBL."

"No fucking way."

Charlie was right the whole time. I couldn't believe it.

Now all of the talk from the mulch guy made sense. Jay was in D.C. helping plan this mission.

"Yep, UBL," one guy said. "They found him."

"Where?" I said.

"Pakistan."

CHAPTER 10
The Pacer

They led me into a conference room that served as the operations center.

Laptops and printers were set up on folding tables. Maps of Pakistan hung on one wall, including maps of a city called Abbottabad. All of the furniture was made of faux leather, with under-stuffed cushions and metal armrests. The guys had pushed most of the lounge furniture to one side next to the plastic plants to make room for gear.

The room was empty except for a few civilians from the CIA working quietly. I tried to take in some of the maps and photographs, but it was all so overwhelming. I still couldn't believe they finally found Osama bin Laden.

We had never had any good leads. He was like a specter hanging over the whole war. We all dreamt about being on the mission to kill or capture him, but no one really thought about it seriously. There was too much luck involved. We all knew it came down to being in the right place at the right time, and walking into the operations center that Tuesday it appeared we were all in the right place. They had simply handpicked the most senior guys in the squadron rather than pull an existing troop.

Mike walked up and saw us in front of the organizational chart. There were twenty-eight names on the list, including an EOD tech. An interpreter and a combat assault dog, named Cairo, rounded out the team.

"Ali is a terp from the agency," Mike said. "Terp" was short for interpreter. There would also be four alternates in case someone got hurt in training. "We broke everything down into four teams, and I've got you down as one of the four team leaders."

Tom was also listed as a team leader.

"You'll be on Chalk One for the infil," Mike said. "Your team is responsible for the guesthouse, C1, to the south."

C1 was the designation for the guesthouse, a separate structure from the main house in the compound, which was where Bin Laden would most likely be living. Chalk One and Chalk Two referred to the two helicopters that would carry us on the mission.

I noticed Charlie and Walt were also in Chalk One, but on a different team. The mission was organized so that both helicopters had the same capabilities. Chalk One mirrored Chalk Two. I had an officer on my team who would step in if

Jay's bird went down. Mike, our master chief, counted as part of my team, but once on the ground he was there to direct traffic and keep us on the timeline.

The layout of the target was still unfamiliar. I could see a diagram on one wall showing the compound and the arrow-like shape of its walls. I knew the guesthouse was a peripheral assignment; I'd be lying if I told you for a split second I didn't wish I was going to be part of the team that was tasked with going to the roof of the main building, called A1. If all went as planned they would be the first team to make entry into the third floor, where Bin Laden was thought to be living. That wish quickly faded and I focused on what I was tasked with. There was plenty of action to go around, and I was just happy to be a part of the mission.

"Check," I said, studying the chart. "Is Will coming back for this?"

Will rounded out my team. He was assigned to our sister squadron, which was already based in Jalalabad, Afghanistan. A self-taught Arabic speaker, Will would be able to communicate with Bin Laden's family.

"You'll link up with Will in J-bad," Mike said. "I've got a meeting now, but check out the model. They spent good money on this thing. The rest of the guys should be back from breakfast in a few minutes."

I walked out of the operations center and poked around the building, sipping a coffee. Our equipment was strewn all over the floor in a room just off the foyer. Pelican cases with weapons were open in one corner. Radios on chargers lined the far wall next to bags of tools. A chart printer was pushed into one corner. Crowding another corner were several white boards and easels with writing pads attached for note taking.

I found the mock-up of Bin Laden's compound just outside the doors to the main briefing room. It sat on a five foot by five foot plywood base. It was made of foam; a massive wooden box secured by several padlocks sat in the corner of the room. The box covered the model when it wasn't being used.

The model showed Bin Laden's house in amazing detail, right down to the small trees in the courtyard and cars in the driveway and on the road that ran along the north side of the compound. It also had the location of the compound's gates and doors, water tanks on the roof, and even concertina wire running along the top of the wall. Grass covered the main courtyard. Even the neighbors' houses and fields were rendered in almost exact detail.

Between sips of coffee, I studied the three-story house.

The one-acre compound was on Kakul Road in a residential neighborhood in the city of Abbottabad. The town, north of Islamabad, Pakistan's capital, was named for British major James Abbott. It is the home of Pakistan's military academy.

My other teammates were still eating breakfast, so I had the model to myself. I was eager to get started, but I was still trying to wrap my head around what I learned that morning. We were finally going after Osama bin Laden.

Osama bin Laden was born March 10, 1957, in Riyadh. He was the seventh of fifty children. His father, Mohammed Awad bin Laden, was a construction billionaire, and his mother, Alia Ghanem from Syria, was his father's tenth wife. Bin Laden barely knew his father. His parents divorced when he was ten years old. His mother married again, and he grew up with four stepsiblings.

In high school in Jeddah, Saudi Arabia, Bin Laden joined an Islamic study group that memorized the entire Koran. In high school, he was exposed to fundamentalist Islam and Bin Laden grew his beard long like the Prophet Muhammad.

Bin Laden married his cousin when he was eighteen years old. They had a son in 1976, the same year Bin Laden graduated. He went to King Abdulaziz University in Jeddah and earned a degree in public administration.

When the Soviet Union invaded Afghanistan in 1979, Bin Laden relocated to Peshawar, Pakistan, and later Afghanistan. As a Muslim, it was his duty to fight the invading Soviets, he claimed. He built camps and trained mujahedeen, sometimes using aid from the United States. When the war ended in 1989, Bin Laden returned to Saudi Arabia, but was disgusted by what he considered the corrupt royal government. In 1992, he spoke out against the Saudi government and was banished to Sudan.

A year later, he formed al Qaeda, meaning "the foundation" or "the base" in Arabic. His goal was to start a war with the United States to rally Muslims to create a single Arab country across the Middle East.

His war against the United States started in 1996 when al Qaeda blew up a truck in Saudi Arabia, killing U.S. troops stationed there. Under pressure from the international community, the Sudanese government exiled him, and Bin Laden fled to Afghanistan and the protection of the Taliban.

In 1998, al Qaeda became a household name when his group bombed U.S. embassies in Kenya and Tanzania. The attacks killed close to three hundred people. He followed up the embassy attacks by bombing the USS *Cole* in Aden harbor in 2000. But his most decisive blows were the four attacks on September 11, 2001. His followers killed almost three thousand civilians in New York, Washington, and Pennsylvania. After Coalition forces toppled the Taliban in 2001, Bin Laden went into hiding after narrowly escaping capture by Coalition forces at Tora Bora in Afghanistan.

For the last ten years, Coalition forces, including the United States, had been hunting for him along the Afghanistan-Pakistan border. Besides the 2007 spin-up, all of the intelligence we received had him hiding in Pakistan.

Soon, my teammates started to come in from breakfast. I was still studying the model when Tom walked into the room. He was one of the team leaders on Chalk One, and his team was responsible for clearing the first floor of the main building, called A1.

"They call him the Pacer because he walks for hours. They

keep seeing the Pacer there," Tom said as he pointed to a courtyard on the east side of the compound. "According to what the intel folks are saying, he walks out in the garden area to exercise from time to time. They think the Pacer is UBL."

Walt and Charlie came in next. They both had big grins on their faces.

"You called it," I said to Charlie. "How did they find him?"

"One of his couriers," Charlie said. "He has two guys working for him."

The day before, the CIA had briefed my teammates on the "Road to Abbottabad," essentially how they found Bin Laden. In the operations center, there were several booklets full of intelligence about the area and Bin Laden. While we waited for the others to arrive from breakfast, I started to read the briefings. I was a day behind and wanted to get up to speed before the serious planning started.

Public sources later confirmed that the target compound, worth close to $1 million, was built in 2005, close to Pakistan's military academy. It was much larger than other houses in the area and didn't have a telephone or an Internet connection. The walls were built higher on the southern side of the compound to prevent people seeing inside the courtyard. Those walls blocked the view of the second and third floors. The windows on both the second and third floors of the main building were blacked out so no one could see in or out.

There was no evidence the Pacer had any contact outside

of the compound. The residents burned their trash and had very little contact with their neighbors.

One of the people known to live at the compound was Ahmed al-Kuwaiti.

The CIA learned of Ahmed al-Kuwaiti after the interrogation of a man named Mohammed al-Qahtani, a Saudi citizen and the alleged twentieth hijacker on September 11, 2001. Immigration agents barred him from entering the United States in August 2001 because they thought he was trying to immigrate illegally to the United States. Investigators found out later that Mohammed Atta, one of the leaders of the plot, was waiting for him at the Orlando airport that day.

Al-Qahtani was sent back to Dubai only to get captured in the Battle of Tora Bora in December 2001 and sent to the prison at Guantanamo Bay, Cuba. When his fingerprints came back as the same man sent back by immigration, interrogators went to work over several months in 2002 and 2003.

Al-Qahtani eventually told them that Khalid Sheikh Mohammed, the planner of the September 11 attacks, sent him to the United States. He also admitted to meeting Bin Laden and receiving terrorist training, and identified a man named Ahmed al-Kuwaiti as one of Bin Laden's couriers and right-hand men. Khalid Sheikh Mohammed, who was by this time in American custody as well, also acknowledged he knew al-Kuwaiti, but stressed that the courier was not part of al Qaeda.

Then in 2004, Hassan Ghul was captured. Ghul was a courier and al Qaeda agent. He told intelligence officials al-Kuwaiti was close to Bin Laden. When interrogators questioned Khalid

Sheikh Mohammed about it again, he downplayed al-Kuwaiti's role. Mohammed's successor, Abu Faraj al-Libi, captured by the Pakistanis in 2005, told interrogators he hadn't seen al-Kuwaiti in a while. Since both Mohammed and al-Libi dismissed al-Kuwaiti's role when asked about him, intelligence analysts began to believe he might be with Bin Laden.

The CIA knew that al-Kuwaiti and his brother, thirty-three-year-old Abrar Ahmed al-Kuwaiti, had worked for Bin Laden in the past. The agency started to track Ahmed al-Kuwaiti in Pakistan, hoping he would lead them to his brother and then to Bin Laden.

Then, during an intercepted call to his family in 2010, one of his family members asked him what he was doing for work. For the most part, al-Kuwaiti had been savvy and kept his employer secret. So, when the family member asked what he was doing for work, al-Kuwaiti said he was "doing what he used to do."

That subtle answer connected some dots and provided a good starting point for this operation. It was all circumstantial evidence, but it was all we had to go on.

The CIA started to track Ahmed al-Kuwaiti, watching his patterns. They noticed he drove a white truck with a picture of a rhino on the spare-tire cover. The CIA eventually tracked the truck back to the compound in Abbottabad, which now sat in model-form in front of me.

———

The CIA assessment said Bin Laden lived on the third floor of A1, the main building. His son Khalid lived on the second floor. The CIA expected at least one or two wives and a dozen kids. Kids are typically found at most targets we assault so this was an issue we were very familiar with.

Jay and Mike had helped plan the mission's broad strokes in Washington weeks before, but it was our job to get into the weeds and really put the plan to the test. We knew our capabilities better than anyone, and since we were being trusted to execute the operation we would also have a critical role in the planning.

We all gathered around the model, as Jay and Mike started talking about where the planning was to date. Since the guys had been at it for twenty-four hours, the broad strokes of the plan had started to come together.

"We're going to fly to the X," Jay said. "Chalk One will rope into the courtyard."

Moving over to the south side of the model, Jay pointed at the guesthouse, designated C1.

"Mark, you and your crew are responsible for C1," Jay said. "Your team will move directly to the guesthouse. The sniper will clear the carport and then set up on the roof. You guys will clear and secure C1. Ahmed al-Kuwaiti lives in the house with his wife and kids. When you're finished, move to backfill Tom's team in A1."

The remaining assaulters in Chalk One, led by Tom, would split up and make their way to A1.

"Charlie and Walt will move to the north door of A1 and

wait," Jay said. "They think the Pacer typically uses that door. The CIA's assessment says there is likely a spiral staircase that leads up to his living quarters on the third floor."

Tom and his team would move to the southern door, enter, and clear the first floor. The courier's brother, Abrar Ahmed al-Kuwaiti, was thought to live on the first floor of the building with his family. Based on what Tom saw inside, his team would either clear through to the north door or let Charlie and Walt in. If blocked, they would exit and loop around to the north door.

"We have no idea of the layout inside the house other than we suspect that the house is cut into two living areas," Jay said. "So Charlie and Walt will hold their position until Tom gives them the all-clear to breach."

Meanwhile, the second helicopter—carrying Chalk Two—would drop off a five-person team north of the compound that would act as external security. Two assaulters and the CAD (combat assault dog) would patrol the perimeter of the compound. The dog would be used to track down squirters. The remaining two assaulters and the interpreter would position themselves just to the northeast corner of the compound to deal with possible onlookers or local police.

This external security job was actually one of the biggest and most dangerous positions on the raid. If we ran long on target, they would have to deal with first responders, most likely police, and the threat of military forces showing up. It wasn't the sexy mission, but it was absolutely essential and could end up being the most dynamic.

"Once outer security is dropped off, the helo will pick up and hover above A1 and the remaining assaulters are going to rope onto the roof, make their way down onto the third-floor balcony, and clear the third deck."

If the intelligence was correct and everything went according to plan, that was the team that was most likely to encounter Bin Laden first.

The rest of the brief Jay and Mike spent going over the load plan. Finally they designated several "pro" words for the operation. Pro words are one-word messages that relay information in an efficient manner. This kept radio traffic to a minimum and made passing information more reliable. On this mission, we chose pro words with a Native American theme.

"UBL is Geronimo," Jay said.

The mission briefing took about an hour, and when we were done Mike and Jay left.

"Now you guys shoot holes in this," Mike said. "Jay and I have been looking at this for several weeks now. You guys got it yesterday. Take some time and really get into the weeds."

We tried never to fall in love with a plan, because that breeds complacency.

The first thing we tried to do was find an alternate way to approach the target. No one wanted to fly to the X. We'd given up doing that years ago. We were more comfortable being dropped off and patrolling to the compound. Our tactics had evolved over the years into being as sneaky as we could so we could keep the element of surprise until the very last second.

The reconnaissance and sniper teams studied satellite images, trying to find landing zones within four to six kilometers of the target, but none of the routes seemed to work. The compound was in a residential area. All of the landing zones were either too close to urban areas or we'd have to walk down city streets. The risks of getting compromised during our infil were too high. In the end, flying to the X was the lesser of two evils. It would be loud, but it would be fast. We couldn't risk being compromised during the foot patrol.

Huddled in separate corners of the operations center, the teams got together individually to plan their part. Beyond our personal gear, we started to divide up our team gear list—a ladder, a sledgehammer, and explosives.

"I'll need the ladder to climb the carport," the sniper said. The collapsible ladder was heavy and burdensome. "Mike said he'd carry it on his back during the fast-rope so I can provide better security."

We positioned two snipers, one in each door of Chalk One, to cover us as we roped into the compound. We didn't need someone walking into the compound with an AK-47 and shooting us as we slid down the rope.

"Since Will isn't here to argue, he gets the sledge," I said with a smirk. "I'll carry two breaching charges and a set of bolt cutters."

A breaching charge was a two-inch-thick strip of explosives. The charge was about twelve inches long with a strip of adhesive that ran along its spine so we could stick it to the door. Once initiated, it would explode in about three seconds and usually tear a door open by cutting through the locking mechanism.

The goal of each team was to be self-sufficient. The last thing anybody wanted was to have to call another team over to help because they didn't have the right equipment.

A woman from the National Geospatial-Intelligence Agency, a blonde in her early thirties, took care of the maps and satellite images for us. She provided any detail—big or small.

Kneeling down to look at the mock-up, I studied the door leading into the guesthouse.

"Hey, are these doors on C1 inward or outward opening?" I asked her.

She was back in a few minutes with the answer.

"Double metal door," she said. "Opens outwards."

It was like that all week. If we had a question, they had the answer, including where the Pacer walked, who else lived on the compound, which gates were locked or unlocked, and even where they frequently parked their cars. They had a huge number of images from drones and satellites, and there wasn't much they didn't know about the outside environment of the compound.

In Washington, President Obama and his advisors were still discussing different options. The president still had not signed off on the ground-assault option. All we had been authorized to do up to now was to start planning and conduct rehearsals. The White House was still considering an Air Force option, a massive air strike using B-2 Spirit bombers to level the house.

Defense Secretary Robert Gates supported the air strike because it kept American ground forces out of Pakistan, which made the mission less like an invasion of the country's sovereignty.

The United States didn't have a great track record when it came to commando raids like the one we were planning. Since Operation Eagle Claw, there was a lot of risk in putting troops in harm's way in a sovereign country.

During Eagle Claw, one of six helicopters flying to a desert staging base in Iran before the raid hit a fierce sand cloud and crashed into an MC-130E containing fuel. The fire destroyed both aircraft and killed eight servicemen. The mission, one of the first operations conducted by Delta Force, was aborted. Eagle Claw was a disaster and contributed to Carter losing his reelection campaign.

The air-strike option required thirty-two two-thousand-pound smart bombs. The barrage would last for a full minute and a half and the crater would penetrate at least thirty feet into the earth in case the compound had a bunker system. The possibility for collateral damage was high, and the possibility of finding identifiable remains after that kind of destruction was low.

If we were going to conduct this mission either with an air strike or raid, they wanted proof it was Bin Laden. The assault was risky, but the air strike added additional complications.

———

A few days after we arrived in North Carolina, we saw the Pacer for the first time.

Standing around the computer screen, we watched drone footage of the compound. The feed was black-and-white with little detail. I could make out the main building and the courtyard that took up the northeastern part of the compound.

After a few seconds, I saw the Pacer enter the frame. From the video feed, he looked like an ant. There was no way we could make out his face or even how tall he was. But we could see him walk out of the north door and start pacing in an oval clockwise around the courtyard. A makeshift awning was rigged up to cover him, but it only shaded part of the garden.

"He does this for hours," one of the agency analysts said. "I've seen him walk by guys doing work, but he never helps. He just paces."

Sometimes, he walked with a female or a child. None of them stopped to do any work. When a veterinarian came to treat the cow that lived in the courtyard, they moved it to another courtyard for treatment.

"We believe the reason they moved the cow is they don't want anyone to see that side of the compound," the analyst said. "It's circumstantial, but it looks like they are hiding someone. Hey, take a look at this."

Clicking to another day's feed, we could see the compound and then, from the right side of the screen, a Pakistani helicopter flew over.

"Where did that come from?" I said.

"A PakMil Huey," the analyst said. "Not sure where it came from, but it was leaving the military academy."

We all stared at the screen, waiting to see if anyone in the compound reacted. We didn't see the Pacer sprint to a car and run. Instantly, we all thought the same thing. This meant he was accustomed to hearing helicopters.

"We might actually be able to get on the deck before they really figure out what is going on," Charlie said.

With the mission planned out, we began rehearsals.

The Black Hawk swooped over the North Carolina pine forest and came to a hover over the compound. From my perch, sitting legs blowing in the breeze just outside the left door of the helicopter, I could see the life-size mock-up of Bin Laden's compound. Nestled in a remote part of the base, the practice compound was built to scale using plywood, chain-link fence, and shipping containers.

Sliding down the fast-rope, I landed in the courtyard and moved to the double doors at C1. All around me, my teammates were racing to their objectives. The roar of the engines above us made it hard to talk, but after three days of practice we didn't need to talk. The whole mission had become muscle memory. Besides some time hacks that were called out over the radio, the net was silent. Everyone knew their individual jobs. We had years and years of experience among the groups, so everything moved smoothly. This target wasn't any more complicated than hundreds of others we'd assaulted over the years.

The rehearsals were less about training and more about selling to the White House that we could do it.

The level of detail on the mock-up was impressive. The construction crews at the base had planted trees, dug a ditch around the compound, and even put in mounded dirt to simulate the potato fields that surrounded the compound in Pakistan.

After a few runs, we asked if they could add the third-floor balcony and move some of the gates to better simulate the layout of the actual compound.

Before the next rehearsal, the changes were made.

The construction crew didn't ask why and never said no. They just showed up and made all requested changes. We'd never been treated like this. All of the bureaucracy was gone. If we needed something, we got it. No questions asked. It was a far cry from what we were forced to deal with in Afghanistan.

The only black hole in the practice compound was the interiors. We had no idea what the inside of the house looked like. It wasn't a big concern. We had years of combat experience, and we could apply it to this problem. We had no doubt we could pull this off; we just needed to get on the ground.

Stopping at the door of the container that simulated C1, I scanned inside before entering. During the real mission, I had no idea if Ahmed al-Kuwaiti would be armed or if he had a suicide vest. We anticipated all of the men—Bin Laden, Khalid, and the two Kuwaiti brothers—would fight back.

After we rehearsed the best-case scenario, we started running through the contingencies. Instead of roping into the courtyard, we landed outside the walls and raided the compound from there. We also practiced tracking down squirters if someone ran from the target before the assault.

Every single contingency was practiced to the point where we were tired of it. We had never trained this much for a particular objective before in our lives, but it was important. The mission was straightforward, but the extra preparation helped us mesh, since we'd been drawn from different teams.

After the last rehearsals, we all met in the operations center. Jay was there with an update.

"We're headed home and then Monday we head out west for another week of training and a full mission profile," he said.

I raised my hand.

"Do we have any official word if this thing is approved yet or not?" I said.

"Nope," he said. "Still waiting on Washington."

I looked at Walt. His eyes rolled. It was the "hurry up and wait" routine we had experienced with the Captain Phillips operation.

"My money says we don't launch," Walt said as we left.

———

We flew out to our training site early Monday. On Thursday, almost two weeks after we got the initial tasking, we had our dress rehearsal.

The entire team and all the planners gathered in a massive hangar at the base. On the floor was a map of eastern Afghanistan. A group of VIPs, headlined by Admiral Mike Mullen, the chairman of the Joint Chiefs, and Admiral Eric Olson, commander of the Special Operations Command in Tampa and a former DEVGRU commander, sat in stands near the map with Vice Admiral Bill McRaven.

McRaven has commanded at every level within the special operations community, including DEVGRU. He impressed me. McRaven, the three-star admiral atop the Joint Special Operations Command (JSOC), was tall, lean, and clean-cut. Most admirals look old or out of shape, but McRaven looked like he could still get the job done. He knew how to work his level and had a good handle on the politics in D.C.

We were about to execute what was called a "rock drill," and everything from helicopter flight paths to the mock-up of the compound was present on the floor. A narrator reading off a script started the hour-and-a-half-long brief on Operation Neptune Spear.

The pilots spoke first. They walked everyone through the flight path from Jalalabad to the compound in Abbottabad. They talked about the radio calls as well as any contingencies that might arise in flight.

Finally, each assault team leader got up and briefed their individual tasks.

"My team will fast-rope from Chalk One into the courtyard, we'll clear and secure C1, then backfill the rest of the teams in A1," I said.

Most of the questions from the VIPs focused on the perimeter team. There were a lot of concerns about how our external security would handle onlookers.

"What is your plan if you're confronted by local police or military?" they asked the team leader.

"Sir, we will de-escalate if at all possible," he said. "First using the interpreter, and then using the dog, and then visible lasers. As a last resort we will use force."

Toward the end, a question was raised about whether or not this was a kill mission. A lawyer from either the Department of Defense or the White House made it clear this wasn't an assassination.

"If he is naked with his hands up, you're not going to engage him," he told us. "I am not going to tell you how to do your job. What we're saying is if he does not pose a threat, you will detain him."

After the brief, we loaded up into the helicopters and took off for one final run-through. We were going to assault a mock compound so the VIPs could watch. It was the final hurdle. I knew we had to do it, but it felt strange to be watched like this. It felt like we were in a fish bowl. We all agreed if jumping through these hoops was going to help us get approval, the hassle was worth it.

One minute from the target, the crew chief threw open the door and I swung my legs out.

Grabbing the rope, I could see some VIPs near the target staring up at us with night vision goggles. As the helicopter started its hover over our fast-rope location, the rotors kicked up a maelstrom of rocks and dust, blasting the VIPs and forcing them to run in the opposite direction. I chuckled as I watched a few of the women stagger away on their heels.

The rehearsal went off without an issue on our end.

"So, you think we'll get the go-ahead?" Charlie asked me after the dress rehearsal.

"Dude, I've got no clue," I said. "I'm not holding my breath."

The flight back the next day was low-key. We were ready to go. There was nothing we could do now but wait.

CHAPTER 11

Killing Time

The sun was fading as I flashed my ID card to the guard at our base in Virginia Beach. He saw my decal as I pulled closer and waved me through. I passed a long line of cars heading home for the day.

I was a few hours early for our flight, but I was tired of waiting. It had been a long week at home. When we are home too long, we get antsy. It was Easter, and I called my parents to check in. We caught up, but I couldn't tell them what I was really doing. While the rest of America was coloring Easter eggs, we were sitting on the biggest secret of our lives.

After the dress rehearsal out west, it all came down to the politicians in Washington making a decision. We made one more trip to North Carolina to conduct a last walk-through of the compound, before returning to find out we'd finally gotten orders to move forward and stage in Jalalabad, Afghanistan.

We were all still very skeptical. Nobody was jumping up and down; everybody digested the news in their own way and went about their business. At least we were one step closer to actually roping into the compound.

I parked my truck and grabbed my backpack. I could see some of my teammates walking toward the headquarters. I'm sure we all had the same thoughts running through our minds.

"Holy shit, I can't believe they actually approved this."

I think most of us were convinced there was no way this was actually going to happen. In a way, it's a defense mechanism. That way, if it got turned off at the last minute, we wouldn't be too upset.

"Yeah, whatever. I'll believe it when we are airborne," Walt said, walking with me into the lobby of the building.

"This has a good chance if they are actually sending us over," I said.

By moving us, they risked more and more leaks. The rest of our command definitely knew something was going on. Even a troop movement of this relatively small size could cause spikes when a bunch of operators came through Bagram on a non-scheduled rotation.

Inside the team room, guys were eating a last-minute snack before the long flight. Some just stood around talking. We were all dressed in jeans and button-up collared shirts, our normal travel attire. We looked like a bunch of guys going on vacation. If we'd been carrying golf clubs instead of rifles and night vision goggles, you might mistake us for a professional sports team.

Other than my equipment for the raid itself, I was traveling light, with only a few changes of clothes, my shower kit, and flip-flops. We weren't staying long. The plan was to fly over, spend two days getting acclimated, and conduct the mission on the third night.

Buses soon took us from our base to a nearby airport. On the tarmac sat a massive gray C-17 Globemaster. Its engines idled as the Air Force crew did pre-flight checks. Already on board were the helicopter mechanics. Nearby, a group of National Security Agency and CIA analysts kept to themselves.

As we sat down, it felt comfortable, like a place we'd been many times before. This was the same way we always went on deployment. Inside the belly of the aircraft, our equipment and the helicopter crews' tools were strapped to the deck. Seats lined the walls. I threw my backpack on the deck and fished out my nylon green jungle hammock. Looking around the cargo bay for a place to hang it, I saw my teammates crawling around the plane like ants looking for a comfortable spot to stretch out. We were experts in making the flight as comfortable as possible.

I attached my hammock between two containers holding gear. Other guys claimed spots on top of containers or in the open space between the seats and the cargo. Some of my teammates pumped up camping mattresses, but I was one of the few who used the hammock. It was issued to us for jungle missions, but I liked that it kept me off the cold floor.

We had a nine-hour flight to Germany and after a short layover another eight hours to get to Bagram. Getting as much sleep as we could on the flight was imperative.

The Air Force crew chased us back to our seats to strap in just before takeoff. The only open seat was next to Jen, a CIA analyst. Slipping the buckle of my seatbelt into the clasp, I felt the plane start to taxi to the end of the runway. Minutes later, we raced down the tarmac and quickly climbed into the sky. Once we were level, guys started to pop Ambien and settle in for the long flight.

I wasn't tired, so I started to talk with Jen. I'd seen her around in North Carolina, but we hadn't gotten to talk at length since we started planning the operation. I was curious to get her take on things since she was one of the leading analysts that helped in the hunt for Bin Laden.

"Honestly," I asked Jen. "What are the odds it's him?"

"One hundred percent," she shot back, almost defiant.

Recruited by the agency out of college, she'd been working on the Bin Laden task force for the last five years. Analysts rotated in and out of the task force, but she stayed and kept after it. After the al-Kuwaiti phone call, she'd worked to put all the pieces together. I missed the first day's brief, where Jen laid out how they tracked him to Abbottabad. In the weeks since, she had been our go-to analyst on all intelligence questions regarding the target.

We'd heard the "one hundred percent" call in the past, and each time it made my stomach hurt.

"Be careful with that shit," I said. "When our intel folks say it is one hundred percent it, is more like ten. When they say ten percent, it is more like one hundred."

She smiled, undeterred.

"No, no," Jen said. "One hundred percent."

"One hundred percent like in 2007," I said.

Like me, she remembered 2007, when we'd been spun up to chase the guy in white flowing robes. Jen rolled her eyes and frowned.

"That wasn't a good lead," she said, even though the lead had come from a CIA source. "That whole thing spun out of control quickly."

It was nice to hear the CIA take even some of the blame, although you could pretty much throw a stick in 2007 and hit someone responsible for that debacle. That mission had been weighed down by the typical problem of everybody wanting to be involved. Already, the differences between 2007 and now were apparent, which lent more credibility to the current mission.

Jen wasn't afraid to share her opinion with even the highest officers, including Vice Admiral McRaven. She had made it known in the beginning that she was not a fan of the ground-assault option.

"Sometimes JSOC can be the big gorilla in the room," she said. "I'd rather just push the easy button and bomb it."

This was a typical attitude outside of JSOC. There were a lot of haters not only from the big military side but also from the agency. Not everyone trusted us, because they didn't know us.

"Don't hold back," I said. "Love us or hate us, you're in the circle of trust now. We're all in this together."

"You mean the boys' club," Jen said. "You guys are just showing up for the big game."

She was right. This was her baby. Jen and her team spent five years tracking him to get us to where we were now. We were just here to finish the job.

"You guys did all the hard work to get us here," I said. "We're happy to have our thirty minutes of fun and be done."

"I'll admit, you guys aren't what I was expecting at all," she said.

"See, I told you you're in the circle," I said.

It was dark when we landed in Bagram. We taxied to a spot far from the main terminals at the base, the ramp opened, and we saw a C-130 with its ramp down and props turning. Bagram is the main NATO base in northern Afghanistan. A massive base just north of Kabul, it had grown into the size of a small city. Thousands of soldiers and civilian contractors called the base home. Little fighting occurred out of Bagram. In fact, it had gotten so safe that now the only danger was getting a ticket for speeding on the base's streets or for not wearing a reflective belt at night. Spending any time at Bagram would make it tough to keep our secret.

Thankfully, we were headed to Jalalabad. The runway there was too small and couldn't handle C-17s. JSOC arranged the C-130 to meet us. We didn't want to risk going to the main Bagram terminal or the chow hall and being seen. A whole troop showing up out of cycle would raise questions.

Gathering our bags and shaking off the Ambien, we walked silently off the back of the C-17 and directly onto the C-130.

While we settled into the orange nylon jump seats that were hung near the front of the plane, Air Force ground crews strapped three of the containers with our gear into the back of the plane. The ramp closed, and we made the one-hour flight to the base in J-bad.

The seats on the C-130 were uncomfortable. If you get stuck in the middle row, you have to rely on the guy behind you to sit up, providing support, or you sink down, crushing your back. If being able to lay out in a hammock in a C-17 was first-class military flying, then the middle seat in a C-130 was economy.

Landing in a C-130, even on a paved runway, was jarring. The wheels are close to the fuselage, so it was like landing a roller skate. Plus, it sounded like the plane itself was hitting the tarmac. I held on to the bar as the plane swung around and stopped at the main terminal. The crew chief lowered the gate, revealing buses waiting to take us to the JSOC compound.

Jalalabad airfield is located just a few miles from the Pakistan border. Home to a number of American units, including a force from JSOC, the base is the main staging area for helicopters operating in northeastern Afghanistan.

Larger than the smaller outposts that dot the valleys along the border, Jalalabad is part of Regional Command East and it's from J-bad that units along the border get supplies and mail. It is home to about fifteen hundred soldiers as well as a number of civilian contractors. Afghan security forces help guard the base.

The runway splits the base in half. Soldiers live on the south side of the airfield. The JSOC area had its own chow hall, gym, operations center, and a number of plywood huts. The compound was home to Army Rangers, DEVGRU, and support personnel.

Almost all of us had double-digit deployments to J-bad. Walking through the gate, it felt like home.

"What's up, brother?" Will said to me when we arrived.

He'd already gotten word that he would be part of the raid, and he was eager to get read in on the plan.

After putting our gear away, we met back at the fire pit. Guys on previous rotations had built the brick-and-mortar pit, which had become a de facto town square for the compound. Each deployment we added to it until it looked like the patio of a fraternity house. Shitty couches purchased out in town were usually crowded with guys drinking coffee, smoking cigars, or just bullshitting. The couches rotated as often as we did. Made in Pakistan, the cheap stuffing in the cushions couldn't handle our two-hundred-pound frames for long.

The SEALs already on their scheduled deployment in Ja-lalabad got briefed on the plan during our flight over. They heard rumors something was spinning up, but no one knew any details until the brief.

Because Will spoke Arabic, he was the only member of his squadron selected to go with us on the assault. The rest of his teammates would be the quick reaction force or QRF, loaded in two CH-47 helicopters waiting to be called in to help if the team at the compound ran into trouble. They were also tasked to set up a forward air refueling point (FARP) north of the compound. Using the massive CH-47 helicopters, which were basically flying school buses, the QRF would carry inflatable fuel bladders so the Black Hawks carrying the assault teams could stop for much-needed gas on the return flight to Jalalabad.

"You seen the mock-up?" I asked Will.

We went into a briefing room near the operations center and I undid the padlocks. Will helped me lift the wooden cover off.

"Wow. This is nice," he said, leaning over it to look closely at the mock-up.

Will looked like your average SEAL. He was about five foot ten inches tall with a lean physique. The thing that made him different was the fact that he had taught himself Arabic. He was extremely smart, professional, and a man of few words.

The SEAL teams were a very close-knit community. It felt odd showing up to do this mission when everyone knew the squadron that was already deployed could have pulled it off just as well as we could. The only reason we were tasked with this mission was because we were available to conduct the needed rehearsals to sell the option to the decision makers at the White House. Every squadron at the command was interchangeable. It came down to being at the right place at the right time.

"So, give me the rundown," Will said.

"OK, we're in Chalk One," I said. "Our bird will be the first to approach from the southeast and hold station here."

I pointed at the courtyard.

"We'll rope in and clear this building, which we're calling C1," I said.

It was pretty standard stuff, and it didn't take Will long to fall into step. For the next several hours, we went over the whole plan and all the contingencies. I told him about all the rehearsals leading up to this point. This was Will's first taste of the extensive planning the rest of us had been dealing with for weeks. Spending three weeks rehearsing for a mission was very odd. Typically, in Afghanistan or Iraq, we would get tasked with a mission, plan it, and launch in a few hours.

The head shed—our headquarters staff—continued to work on big-picture planning and coordination. With our gear ready, all we had to do was wait.

By rule, most of us had attention deficit disorder, or at least we joked that we did. We could focus on things, but not for long, and waiting was the worst. Walt constantly gave me a hard time. I couldn't even sit through a movie.

Like the other guys, we all had our own method to our madness when it came to how we set up our gear. Everything was checked and then rechecked. All of the batteries in my night vision and laser sights were fresh. My radios sat on the charger. Everything was neatly set out in order. Boots and socks next to my folded uniform. My kit, a vest that held two ballistic plates and pouches for ammunition and gear, rested next to my H&K 416 at the end of my bed.

I took my time laying out my gear, but by midnight, or lunchtime for us, we still had hours to kill. During that kind of downtime, we'd go to the gym. Some guys made coffee, but not instant—French press. One guy brought a Pelican case with a press, grinder, and an assortment of coffees that would make Starbucks blush. I'd catch them making the coffee. One cup could take an hour. They'd grind the beans and then press the coffee. With great care, they'd boil the water and then sit by the fire and sip the coffee. It was all a part of their ritual, and the time they spent obsessing about the coffee meant fewer minutes to sit and wait. Every one of us had developed some method for killing time. We had two days before the mission was scheduled to launch, if it was approved.

The next day, I went with Will and two of his teammates over to the hangar to meet the pilots. We had already worked with the aircrews from the 160th Special Operations Aviation Regiment during our rehearsals.

We worked with the 160th almost exclusively. In our eyes, they were the best pilots in the world.

Teddy, a short, fifty-year-old man with close-cropped hair who was the pilot of Chalk One, met us at the hangar door. We walked around the Black Hawk and showed Will the load plan. Then, before we left, we talked about contingencies.

"If things go bad and I have to make an emergency landing, I am going to do my best to put her down in that open courtyard to the west," said Teddy.

We called it Echo courtyard, and it was the largest open area on the compound. A seasoned pilot, Teddy knew that if his helicopter was hit by enemy fire or malfunctioned, this courtyard was his best option.

"Don't worry though," I said. "We've had our share of wrecks. If anyone is going to crash it will be Chalk Two."

I'd never been in a crash, but seven out of the dozen SEALs on my chalk had been in some form of crash in the past. Only two of the men on Chalk Two's bird could say the same thing. We joked that the law of averages should keep our bird in the air.

The window of opportunity to launch was short. The illumination cycle would start increasing the following week. We wouldn't have these types of optimal conditions again for a month. Plus, with everything in place, the longer we held off, the greater the concern that the mission would leak. In the three weeks since we started planning, the number of people who knew about the operation had expanded exponentially.

JSOC was ramping up its activity. McRaven was in Afghanistan, which isn't news in itself, but the fact that he was heading to J-bad caused a bit of a stir. A Ranger colonel ran daily operations out of our command center in Bagram. Eventually, he was read in on the mission, adding more and more people who knew what was spinning up.

Back in Washington, the main concern seemed to be confidence in the intelligence. Unlike Jen, her fellow analysts were only about sixty percent certain Bin Laden lived in the compound.

In Afghanistan, we were oblivious to the hand-wringing in Washington. We had daily briefings. Drones flew over the compound keeping watch. We also had to battle the "good idea fairy." She shows up on all our missions to some degree or another, and she isn't our friend. The fairy shows up when the head shed has too much time on their hands. Essentially, officers and planners start dreaming up unrealistic scenarios that we may have to deal with on a mission.

"They want us to take a bullhorn for crowd control now," the team leader in charge of outer security said. "This ranks right up there with the police light."

Earlier, the head shed had floated an idea for the outer security team to take one of Bin Laden's cars and affix a police light to it to make the activity around the target look like a police operation.

"So I said, 'Hey, sir, are we just going to push it out there?' We aren't going to have the keys," the team leader said. "What if the steering wheel locks? Plus, which team has time to push a car out of the driveway and all the way down to the street corner? And let's not forget that we will now have a flashing police light highlighting our position."

"What color are police lights in Pakistan?" I said.

"No idea," he said. "That was my next question. Then we got into a half-hour discussion about Ali." Ali was the CIA interpreter on external security. He spoke Pashtun, which was used in the local area. "The good idea fairy wants him in local civilian clothes. He's going to be standing between a SAW gunner and me. We're in uniform, so what does it matter?"

Logic won out in both battles. We didn't carry the police light and Ali was in uniform.

This kind of stuff always happens when planners get into the weeds. The CIA asked us to take a sixty-pound box that blocked cell phone signals. Weight was already an issue, so that good idea died quickly. If we had all the time back we wasted fighting the fairy, we might regain a few years of our lives.

On the second night, I sat at the fire pit sipping on some fresh coffee with Charlie and Walt. The debate of the day was over where in the body you should attempt to shoot Bin Laden.

"Try not to shoot this motherfucker in the face," Walt said. "Everybody is going to want to see this picture."

"But if it's dark and I can only see his head, I'm not waiting for a suicide vest," Charlie said.

"These will be some of the most viewed pictures of all time," I said. "If given the option, all I'm saying is shoot for the chest."

"Easier said than done," Walt said.

"Remember to aim high," I said to Walt. "Since you only come up to his nuts."

We'd already decided that Elijah Wood had Walt's role in the movie, since he was no taller than a hobbit.

Casting the Bin Laden movie was an ongoing joke. Who was going to play whom in Hollywood's version of the mission? No one was getting Brad Pitt or George Clooney. Instead, we had a red-haired guy on the team so Carrot Top would portray him for sure. At least Walt had Frodo instead of a second-rate comic.

"You know if this goes, we'll get Jay his star," I said.

Everyone knew that for the officers, like Jay, if the raid was successful it would be a career maker. It would most likely mean Jay would make admiral some day. For the enlisted guys, it really didn't mean anything; to us it was just another job.

"And we'll get Obama reelected for sure," Walt said. "I can see him now, talking about how he killed Bin Laden."

We had seen it before when he took credit for the Captain Phillips rescue. Although we applauded the decision-making in this case, there was no doubt in anybody's mind that he would take all the political credit for this too.

We all knew this was bigger than us and bigger than politics. Maybe the officers and politicians would benefit, but that didn't make us want to do it any less. That was always how things went. Our reward was doing the job, and we wouldn't have it any other way.

Near dawn, the fire pit broke up and we all went and tried to get a few hours of sleep. Since we operated at night, the majority of the population on the JSOC compound slept all day.

I popped two Ambien. No one was getting any rest without sleeping pills. No matter how much we tried to make this mission just like the others, it wasn't. It had been two days, but it felt like months.

The third day was supposed to be "go day," but cloud cover delayed our launch. No big deal for us. We always get delayed, so we expected it. Getting delayed was better than getting canceled. McRaven wanted to make sure drones could watch the compound in case Bin Laden left while we were in route, and the cloud cover made that impossible.

Our daily briefs were held in a long, narrow room with wooden handmade benches running down the middle like a church. At the front of the room were flat-screen TVs for PowerPoint presentations and to show us drone footage or satellite photos.

Today's briefing was standing room only. I was seated next to Charlie near the back on one of the benches. I saw several of the SEALs from the other squadron wedged around the model, which still demanded your attention when you saw it. They were studying it intently before the briefing. It was amazing how it sucked you in and you'd find yourself fixated on it.

A portion of the briefing was about what to do if the mission went drastically wrong and the Pakistani authorities somehow apprehended us.

The president had already given us the green light to protect ourselves, even if we had to engage the Pakistan military. We were going deep into Pakistan, and we needed a reason other than the truth in case we were detained.

"OK, guys," the officer said. "Here is what they came up with. We're on a search and recovery mission for a downed ISR platform," he said.

An ISR platform is what the military calls a drone. Essentially, we were going to have to tell the Pakistani interrogators that the United States Air Force lost a drone.

We all laughed.

"That is as good as they can come up with?" someone said from the back of the room. "Why don't they give us a bullhorn and a police siren just in case?"

The story was preposterous. We were allies with Pakistan on paper, so if we did lose a drone, the State Department would negotiate directly with the Pakistani government to get it back. The story didn't wash and would be very difficult to stick to during hours of questioning.

At least we could laugh at it. Maybe they figured humor would help us endure. The truth is, if we got to that point, no story we could come up with was going to cover up twenty-two SEALs packing sixty pounds of hi-tech gear on their backs, an EOD tech, and an interpreter for a total of twenty-four men, plus a dog, raiding a suburban neighborhood a few miles from the Pakistani military academy.

At the end of the brief, the commanding officer of DEVGRU came walking in. A captain with silver hair and a mustache, he'd lost his leg in a parachute accident years ago.

As he walked to the front of the conference room, I barely noticed the slight hitch in his step from the prosthetic limb.

The officer briefing us faded into the background as the commander got to the front. All of the laughing and grumbling about the cover story receded, and the room was silent.

"OK, guys," the DEVGRU commander said. "Just got off the phone with McRaven. He just talked to the president. The operation has been approved. We're launching tomorrow night."

There were no cheers or high fives. I glanced back at some of the fellas sitting on the benches around me. The guys I'd operated side by side with for years.

"Holy shit," I thought. "I didn't think it was really going to happen."

No more briefs.

No more good idea fairy.

And most of all, there was no more waiting.

CHAPTER 12

Go Day

I couldn't sleep.

I'd spent the last couple of hours trying to get comfortable. But I found no peace on the hard mattress or in my own head. It was go day, and there was no getting around the significance of the mission now.

Sliding open the camouflage poncho liner hung over my bunk to shield the light, I swung my legs out and rubbed my eyes. After three days of trying not to think about the mission, it was impossible to keep it from my mind now. If everything went as planned, in less than twelve hours we'd be roping into Bin Laden's compound in Pakistan.

I didn't feel tired. The only evidence I'd slept was the

empty baggie that once held a couple of Ambien and a handful of empty bottles now filled with urine. Since we lived in overflow housing, it was a two-hundred-yard walk to the nearest bathroom. So I saved my empty water or Gatorade bottles to piss in instead. Standard practice. We'd flip on our headlamps and relieve ourselves without every truly waking up.

I felt fresh physically, but mentally I was amped up. Not on edge, but restless. The "hurry up and wait" routine was grating on my nerves. We were all just happy the wait was almost over.

Careful to be quiet since some of my teammates were still sound asleep, I slid from the bunk and got dressed. I could hear the faint snores of the others in their rooms. Grabbing my sunglasses, I walked out of the hut and into the daylight. The sun hit me like a sledgehammer. It felt like walking out of a casino in Vegas after playing all night.

It took me a second to adjust, but soon the late afternoon sun felt good on my face and arms as I started walking toward the chow hall. I looked at my watch. For those of us on the compound on vampire hours, it was morning.

For the rest of the base, it was the middle of the workday. The constant roar of helicopters provided the sound track. As I walked, a shit-sucking truck passed by after cleaning a bank of Porta-Johns on the camp. The pungent chemical smell of the disinfectant hung in the air as it passed.

I kept my head down and walked on the gravel that kept the dust down to the first gate. Each unit changed the combination on the gate when they arrived. I fished a slip of paper out of my pocket with the code. My head was still cloudy from the Ambien. Pressing the numbers, I tried the door-knob.

No luck.

It took me three tries to get out, but I was finally on my way.

"Just get through breakfast," I thought.

I was back to surviving Green Team. I knew if you focused on the whole thing, you cracked. The only way to survive was getting through the day one meal at a time. Now, hours before the biggest mission of my career, I was just focused on getting to breakfast.

It was success one step at a time.

Inside the chow hall, I washed my hands under a blast of cold water. The stench of greasy fried cafeteria food was so thick it clung to your clothes. The chow hall still had old holiday decorations pasted on the concrete wall. A long-faded 1970s poster of the four food groups took up most of the bulletin board next to the menu of the day.

I surveyed the long stainless-steel buffets. Behind each one, in an apron and hat, was a civilian contractor ready to serve me a scoop of grits or pile bacon on my plate.

Nothing looked good. The bacon was more fat than meat, and soggy from the grease. But I needed energy. I headed straight for the grill, where a small line was formed. A short-order cook was poised behind the flat top. Scooping up a buttery omelet folded into a greasy mess, he slid it on the plate of the guy in front of me.

"Four eggs," I said as the cook looked at me. "Scrambled please. Ham and cheese."

While the cook started on my eggs, I got some toast and fruit. The selection was the same on every deployment: large trays of unripe dark orange cantaloupe and honeydew with an almost chemical green color. During my last rotation, I had seen a box in the chow hall marked "FOR MILITARY OR PRISON USE ONLY." Seemed about right.

No one joins the military for the food.

I grabbed two pieces of bread and ran them through the restaurant-grade toaster and piled some pineapple onto my plate. You can't screw up pineapple. Back at the grill, I picked up my eggs and stopped to scoop some oatmeal and raisins into a bowl.

I surveyed the tables arranged in long rows in the dining area. The murmur of conversations, coupled with the big-screen TV tucked in the corner tuned to cable news, created a dull roar. I saw a few of my teammates at a table far from the TV and dropped off my tray on my way to get coffee.

The chow hall was for JSOC personnel only, but not everyone knew about the mission.

As I sprinkled some pepper on my eggs, I muttered a hello to my teammates, including Charlie and Tom. They returned the greeting, but like me, no one wanted to talk. We were more comfortable alone with our thoughts.

"How did you sleep?" I said.

"Like shit," Charlie said.

"You take any Ambien?"

"Two," he said.

"Look at the bright side, at least we're enjoying this glorious breakfast. It's like the buffet at Hotel del Coronado."

The hotel was one of the oldest resorts on the Pacific Coast, not far from where we'd all gone through BUD/S.

"Right," Charlie said. "Is that all you can come up with?"

I was trying to be funny, but it was too early. Charlie always gave me shit about my weak jokes. I knew they sucked, but it was part of the fun.

Beyond that, there was no talk of home. No talk of the mission. There was nothing more to cover. The food wasn't good, but you wouldn't have known by looking at our plates when we were through.

I doubt any of us really tasted breakfast. It was just fuel for later. After my eggs and fruit, I forced down the bowl of oatmeal and finished a glass of orange juice. Walking back to my room, I was stuffed. I didn't know when I'd eat next.

The rooms were still quiet when I got back. Some of my teammates were trying to sleep until the last minute, but I was too amped. Getting my toothbrush and a bottle of water, careful not to grab my piss bottle, I walked out to a thick gravel area off to the side and brushed my teeth and spit on the ground.

Breakfast, check.

Brushed my teeth, check.

Back in my room, I stuffed my toothbrush back into my backpack.

I'd already laid out my Crye Precision Desert Digital combat uniform. Designed like a long-sleeved shirt and cargo pants, the uniform had ten pockets, each with a specific purpose. The shirt was designed to wear under body armor. The sleeves and shoulders were camouflaged, but the body of the shirt was tan and made of a lightweight material that wicked sweat away. I'd chopped the sleeves off of my shirt because it was hot.

Sitting on my bed, I started to get dressed. Nothing I did from the moment I started putting on my pants was random.

Every step was carefully planned.

Every check was a way to focus and make sure I didn't forget anything.

These were the same steps I did before every mission.

Before I slid my pants on, I rechecked each pocket on my uniform.

In one cargo pocket, I had my assault gloves and leather mitts for fast-roping. The other cargo pocket had an assortment of extra batteries, an energy gel, and two power bars. My right ankle pocket had an extra tourniquet and my left one had rubber gloves and my SSE kit.

In a pocket on my left shoulder, I felt the $200 cash I'd use if we got compromised and I needed to buy a ride or bribe someone. Evasion takes money, and few things work better than American cash. My camera, a digital Olympus point-and-shoot, was in my right shoulder pocket. Running along the back of my belt, I had a Daniel Winkler fixed blade knife.

I tucked my shirt in and picked up my kit and inspected it again. The ceramic plates covered my vital organs in the front and back. I had two radios mounted on either side of the front plate. Between the radios, I carried three magazines for my H&K 416 assault rifle and one baseball-size fragmentation hand grenade. I also had several chemical lights rigged to the front of my vest, including the infrared version that can only be seen using night vision. We'd crack the plastic lights and throw them in front of rooms and areas that we had cleared. The lights were invisible to the naked eye, but my teammates could see them through their night vision and know what areas were secure.

My bolt cutters rode in a pouch on my back, with the two handles sticking a little ways above my shoulder. Attached to my vest were the two antennas for the radios.

Running my hands over my kit, I tugged on the breaching charge I rubber-banded to the back of it. I next focused on my helmet. It weighed less than ten pounds with the night vision goggles attached. It could officially stop a nine-millimeter round, but in the past the helmets had stopped AK-47 bullets. I switched on the light attached to the rail system that runs down the side of the helmet. It was a brand-new Princeton Tec charge light. I'd used it in my last deployment.

I set the helmet on my head and pulled down my night vision goggles, or NVGs. Unlike some of the conventional units, we had NVGs with four tubes instead of the usual two. This allowed us a field of view of 120 degrees instead of just 40 degrees. The standard goggles were like looking through toilet-paper tubes. Our NVGs allowed us to clear corners more easily and gave us greater situational awareness. Switching on the $65,000 goggles, my room was bathed in a green hue. With a few adjustments, I could see the furniture in crisp detail.

Finally, I picked up my rifle. Pulling it into my shoulder, I turned on my EOTech sight. Mounted behind it was a 3X magnifier, which allowed me to shoot more accurately during the day. Aiming at the wall near my bunk, I tested my red laser, which was visible to the naked eye, and I flipped down my NVGs and tested the IR laser.

Pulling the bolt back, I chambered a round. I performed a press check by sliding the bolt back and inspecting the chamber to make sure a round was seated. I double-checked to make sure it was on safe, and I rested the rifle back against the wall.

With my gear checked and ready, I pulled a small laminated booklet—our cheat sheet for the mission—out of a small pouch in the front of my vest and flipped through it again.

The first page was a mini grid reference guide, or GRG. It was an aerial image of the compound with all of the main areas labeled and the buildings numbered. Everyone worked off the same GRG, from the pilots to the QRF to the people in the operations center.

There was a list of radio frequencies on the following page. The last section had a list of the names and photos of everyone expected on the target. I studied the pictures of the al-Kuwaiti brothers, spending extra time on Ahmed al-Kuwaiti, since he was thought to be living in C1. Each page not only had pictures but also vital stats like height, weight, and any known aliases. The final page had a picture of Bin Laden and several renderings of what he and his son could look like now.

With my camouflage uniform on and my gear ready to go, I grabbed my Salomon Quest boots and pulled them on. They were a little bulkier than the low-top trail-running shoes my teammates sometimes wore. I swore by these boots because they protected my baby ankles, which I twisted with great frequency. I had climbed the mountains in Kunar Province and patrolled through the deserts of Iraq in these boots. All of my gear was proven and had been vetted on previous missions. I knew it all worked.

It finally hit me as I laced up my boots. This could be my last time doing it. What we were about to do was significant. We'd fought hard to keep history out of our minds. We were doing our jobs and this was just the next mission. The task was to assault a house and capture or kill a target. It didn't matter to me who it was supposed to be, but as I tied my laces, it struck me that maybe it did matter. There was no escaping the significance, and I wanted to make sure the laces didn't come undone.

For the last hour, I'd considered the smallest tasks. Everything had to be perfect. I tied the loops of my laces down in a double knot and tucked them into my boot top. In the middle of the room, I hoisted my sixty-pound vest over my head and let it rest on my shoulders. I tightened the straps, basically sealing myself in between the plates. I took a second to make sure I could get to everything. Reaching above my head, I could grab both handles of the bolt cutters. I touched the breaching charge over my left shoulder.

I connected the antennas to my radios and put on my "bone phones," which sat on my cheekbones. These would allow me to hear any radio traffic through bone conduction technology. If I needed, I could also put in an earbud to cancel out the ambient noise and allow sound to travel directly into my ear canal.

In my right ear, I would hear the troop net. On the troop net, I would hear all of my teammates communicating with each other. My left ear would monitor the command net, which would let me communicate with the other team leaders and the head shed.

As a team leader I'd need the two separate nets, but the reality was there wasn't going to be much traffic on the command net for this objective. Only the officers were going to be talking on the satellite radios, and most of the radio traffic on the target would be through the troop net.

All of my checks were done. I'd completed my steps to prepare for the mission. I took one last look in the room to make sure I didn't forget anything, and headed out the door.

The sun was setting. Around me I could hear the others getting ready too. There was little talking, but you could hear guys moving around, checking their equipment or packing up their bags. The door to the building banged against the doorframe with a steady rhythm as guys moved in and out.

We were set to muster at the fire pit in a few minutes. As I got closer, I could hear the thundering beat of a metal band blaring out of some speakers. I met up with my team, and we found a spot and waited for McRaven to show up. He'd requested some time to talk with us before the mission.

"You ready?" I asked Will.

He nodded.

Looking around, I could see Walt, Charlie, and the others waiting with their own teams. Only hours before, we'd been hanging out and laughing about who would play us in the movie. Now, everyone was serious.

McRaven showed up with little fanfare. As he walked up, we all gathered around.

His speech focused on the strategic level, something he was more comfortable talking about. Nothing he said really stuck with me, as my mind was focused on what was about to happen. As he left, word was passed to move out.

"Everybody on the Black Hawks take buses one and two," I heard one of the support guys yell. "Buses three and four are going to the forty-sevens."

The buses were lined up and already running. On board, I wedged myself into a seat near the middle. Will crammed in next to me. The buses were old and dusty. The vinyl seats were worn from years of transporting assaulters in full gear to the flight line.

The bus didn't drive as much as it ambled. The shocks were worn from carrying all the extra weight, so every bump shot through our legs and backs. The ride took only a few minutes, but it felt much longer.

After a while, I could see massive spotlights set up facing outward near the hangar where I knew the Black Hawks waited for us. It looked like a star exploded, and it was impossible to see inside the globe of light. A generator hummed in the background as we got off and walked behind a fence that surrounded the hangar.

Inside, the helicopter crews were making final checks. The noise from the rotors made conversation impossible. I snuck off to the fence to take one last leak. When the helicopters were ready, I saw some of the support crew push open the gate, and the helicopters rolled out.

I nodded to a few guys on Chalk Two, flashing them the middle finger with a smile. We separated in silence. Anything said was lost in the rotor wash, but the gestures all said the same thing.

See you on the ground.

There was nothing more to say.

We formed up on either side of the helicopters. I looked at my watch. We had ten minutes. I found a spot by the tarmac to lie down. I rested my head on my helmet and looked at the stars. For a second, I just relaxed. Finally, the crew chief signaled us to load up.

I was one of the last to get on board, since I would be the first one down the rope. After everyone else had loaded up, there was a small spot by the door, next to Walt and the sniper who would cover us as we fast-roped down. Wedging my ass in as best I could, it was already cramped. I checked my weapon to make sure it was on safe. When you're crammed into a helicopter with little room to move, the last thing you need is for your weapon's safety to get kicked off inadvertently.

I cradled my helmet in my lap to make sure my night vision goggles didn't get damaged. Flipped up, they looked like antlers on the helmet.

Once the door clicked shut, the helicopter picked up and hovered for a few seconds before setting back down. Then, right on schedule, the helicopter leapt from the tarmac. I could feel the nose dip down as we picked up speed. Once we cleared the airfield, the Black Hawk banked to the right and headed for the border.

The cabin was dark and crowded. I could feel Walt's knees dig into my back when he moved. The radio in my ear was silent. I could see a faint glow from the controls in the cockpit, but nothing outside the window. It was pitch-black.

About fifteen minutes into the flight, the first message crackled over the troop net.

"Crossing the border."

"I guess we're actually doing this," I thought.

Soon, my head was bobbing as I dozed. As we got closer to Abbottabad, I could hear the pro words for the different checkpoints come over the troop net. But each time, I slipped back to a light sleep.

"Ten minutes."

That shook me from my daze. I wiped my eyes and wiggled my toes to start working the circulation back. I must have slept more than I thought, since the ten-minute call seemed to come quickly. I think most of the guys on the helicopter actually caught some much-needed sleep on the ride in.

"Six minutes."

All the hype was gone and it was just another night at work for us. I pulled on my helmet and snapped the chinstrap closed. Pulling my NVGs down over my eyes, I made sure everything was in focus. I pulled the gun tightly to my chest so it didn't get hung up when I roped out, and checked the safety one last time. It was still dark in the cabin, but I knew everyone else was making the same checks.

"One minute."

The crew chief slid the door open. I slid the Fast Rope Insertion/Extraction System (FRIES) bar into place. The fast rope was connected to the FRIES bar, which allowed it to fall cleanly to the ground. The bar was held in place with a pin at its base. I ran my hand along the bar and made sure the pin was seated. The crew chief checked it as well. I gave the rope a hard tug to make sure it was secure and then slid my legs out over the edge of the helicopter and into the breeze.

I grabbed the rope and tried to lean out far enough to see ahead of us. Several of the houses we passed over had lighted pools and manicured gardens behind tall stone walls. I was used to seeing mountains or villages made up of clusters of mud huts. From above, Abbottabad reminded me of flying over the suburbs in the United States.

I leaned out the door and finally caught a glimpse of the compound. The flight from Jalalabad had taken about ninety minutes and we would be arriving well after midnight. It was pitch-black and none of the lights in the surrounding houses were on. It seemed like the whole block was without power. Rolling blackouts in the area were common.

The engine noise changed as the helicopter started to hover. Once over the predetermined fast-rope point, I could throw the rope. The hover was rough and it was apparent the pilots were having trouble holding station. It felt like they were wrestling the helicopter, trying to force it to cooperate. My eyes flicked from the ground to the crew chief, waiting for the helicopter to get into position so I could throw the rope.

"GO, GO, GO" ran in a loop in my head.

The pilots never had an issue holding a hover during rehearsals. Something was wrong. We all desperately wanted out of the helicopter and onto the ground.

"We're going around," I heard over the troop net.

"Shit," I thought. "We haven't even gotten on the ground yet and we are already going to plan B."

Suddenly, the helicopter kicked to the right ninety degrees and I could feel my stomach drop like riding a roller coaster. The rotors above me screamed as the Black Hawk tried to claw its way back into the air. With each second, the helicopter slipped closer toward the earth. From my side of the helicopter

I could see the compound rushing up at us through the open door.

I struggled to find a handhold and slide back into the cabin. There was little room behind me as all my teammates had pushed forward prepping to fast-rope. Then I felt Walt's hand grab my gear and pull me deeper into the cabin. His other hand shot out and grabbed the sniper next to me. I leaned back with all my strength. My legs kicked the air as I tried to get them inside. I knew if my legs were exposed when we hit, they would get pinned or cut off.

The closer we got to the ground, the angrier I became. Each and every assaulter had sacrificed so much throughout their individual careers to get to this point. We all felt extremely lucky to have been chosen for this mission and now we were about to die without even getting a chance to do our part.

"Fuck, fuck, fuck," I thought. "This is going to hurt."

CHAPTER 13

Infil

My body was tense and my abs screamed as I tried to fold my legs into my chest.

All I could see was the ground coming up at me through the large open door. Helicopters are not like airplanes that can glide in for a crash landing. When helicopters stop working, they fall out of the sky like a rock. When they hit, rotor blades snap off, sending shrapnel and debris in all directions. Sitting in the open door, I feared the cabin would roll, crushing me underneath.

I could feel Walt tugging on my kit, pulling me back inside the cabin. No matter how much I pulled my legs close, they were still outside the door. The sniper next to me was stuck with one leg inside the cabin and the other outside of it.

It is hard to describe the feeling of riding a helicopter into the ground. I don't think my mind fully grasped what was happening. I had it in my mind that maybe I could stay in the door like a *Looney Tunes* cartoon character. You know, when the house falls off the cliff and the character escapes by opening the front door. For a split second I figured that when the helicopter hit and rolled, I'd land in the door and be safe.

The privacy wall around the compound quickly passed by as we headed for the ground.

When the helicopter rotated ninety degrees, the tail rotor barely missed the wall on the south side of the compound. I could feel fear grip my chest as the ground rushed toward me. I had no control, and I think that scared me most of all. I always figured I would probably die in a gunfight, not in a helicopter crash. We were all used to stacking the odds in our favor. We knew the dangers. We did the battlefield calculus and we trusted our skills. But clinging to a helicopter, there was nothing we could do.

Seconds before impact, I felt the nose dip. I held my breath and waited for impact. The helicopter shuddered as the nose dug into the soft ground like a lawn dart. One minute, the ground was rushing up at me. The next minute, I was at a dead stop. It happened so fast, I didn't even feel the impact.

The blades didn't snap off. Instead, the rotors blasted the muddy courtyard, blowing dust and debris and creating a maelstrom around us.

I exhaled and blinked the dust out of my eyes. Squinting against the assault of rocks and dust, I realized we were still about six feet above the ground at a steep angle.

"Get the fuck out," Walt yelled at me, shoving me forward.

I dropped from the cabin and landed in the courtyard in a crouch. Despite wearing more than sixty pounds of gear, I didn't feel the weight or the jolt from the fall. Without looking back, I ran forward like an Olympic sprinter away from the wreck. Sliding to a halt about thirty yards away, I turned back and saw the wreckage for the first time.

When the helicopter crashed, the tail boom got caught up on the twelve-foot privacy wall. The tail's single load-bearing section propped the Black Hawk up and kept the rotors from hitting the ground. If any other part of the helicopter hit the wall, or if we had tipped and the rotor hit the ground first, none of us would be walking away unscathed. Teddy and his copilot had somehow pulled off the impossible.

I could see my teammates dropping out of the cabin and dashing through a gap underneath the helicopter as it rested at an angle against the wall.

Like my teammates, I had gotten good at compartmentalizing stressful situations over my career, and now I had to block the crash out. Two minutes ago, I was pissed we were going to land outside the compound, but now we were alive and on the ground inside the walls. Despite the near-disaster the mission was still on track.

My teammates were already headed to the gate that led us

back into the main compound. I needed to get my ass in gear because if Charlie or Walt saw me standing there while they were already moving to their positions I would never hear the end of their shit-talking.

We had scheduled thirty minutes to complete the mission based on the helicopter's fuel consumption and a possible response time from the Pakistanis. We had built in an additional ten minutes of flextime just in case. Running back toward the helicopter, I figured we needed those extra minutes now.

The way the helicopter was perched on the wall, I didn't have enough room to clear the rotors in the front. It was dark and even with my night vision it was impossible to be sure how high the rotors were spinning. The only way to get to the compound was by going underneath the wreck.

"I am going explosive," I heard Charlie say over the troop net. I could see him at the gate to the main compound, setting the charge.

Putting my head down, I raced toward the wreck. As I got close, I tried to hug the wall as I ran underneath the tail boom. Hot exhaust blew down from the engines as I passed. It was like walking inside a hair-dryer for a few seconds.

Coming out on the other side, I could see Charlie prepping a charge on the locked iron gate. All around him were guys with their weapons trained out, pulling security.

I moved toward a prayer room near the gate to make sure it was clear. The room had a large open area with thick rugs on the floor and pillows forming a perimeter around the walls.

We knew from the intelligence analysts that the room was most likely used to meet guests, but that seemed to be infrequent. Once cleared, I pulled off an IR chemlight and threw it by the door to alert the others the room was secure.

When I got back outside, Charlie was checking his back blast to make sure no one could get hit by shrapnel from the breaching charge. I saw the quick flash as Charlie hit the detonator and smoothly rolled back out of the way like he had done thousands of times.

We all dipped our heads to protect our eyes. No one was panicked or nervous. We were on the ground and finally it was up to us to get the job done.

The explosion sent a shock wave that blew a hole in the gate. Charlie was the first through, kicking and pulling the scorched metal wider so we could fit. Guys quickly started to pile through and peel off toward their planned objectives. Despite the first few curveballs, we were now back on our original plan.

After clearing the gate, I caught a glimpse of the second Black Hawk carrying Chalk Two. I could tell by the way the helicopter was hovering that Chalk Two had already landed the perimeter security team outside the walls of the compound. From the dozens of times we had trained in the mockup, I was used to getting rotor wash in the face as the helicopter hovered over the building while the teams fast-roped onto the roof.

But instead of hovering above the house, the helicopter quickly disappeared behind the walls. The pilots must have seen us crash, and set back down to drop the team off outside the walls.

"Don't worry about risking a bad position with the helicopters, just get the guys on the ground," Admiral McRaven had reiterated during one of our final briefs. "It doesn't matter where, the most important thing is to get them on the ground safe, and they'll figure out the rest."

I guess Chalk Two hadn't wanted to gamble with fast-roping to the main building after seeing what happened to our helicopter. It was the right call.

I could hear the first few radio calls starting to chime in over the net. I knew from contingency planning that if Chalk Two didn't fast-rope onto the roof, they were headed to a gate on the north side of the compound.

Heading toward C1, Will was next to me as we approached the front door of the guesthouse. The only sound that gave us away was the scuff of our boots on the gravel.

We knew that as one of Bin Laden's most trusted couriers, Ahmed al-Kuwaiti lived in the guesthouse with his family. We expected at least one wife and several children. Since the kids lived there, I didn't expect any booby traps.

Just like on the mock-up and pictures, there was a set of metal double doors with windows at the top. A window on the right side of the door had bars covering the glass. I didn't see any lights on in the house. Sheets covered all of the windows, making it impossible to see inside.

Will took up a position to the left of the door while I tried the knob. I pulled down the L-shaped handle twice, but it was locked.

Stepping back, Will popped his sledgehammer off the back of his kit and pulled out the extendable handle. I covered him from the right.

Will reared back and hit the lock with a sharp whack. The hammer slammed into the knob, but only left a battered handle and a deep gash. Will gave it two more whacks, but nothing budged. The doors were solid metal and we knew the sledgehammer wasn't going to work.

Turning to the windows, Will tried to smash out the glass so we could pull the sheet down and look inside. Wedging the head of the hammer through the bars, he tried to break the panes of glass but each time he pulled back, the head of the hammer got jammed. The bars were just too narrow.

"I am going explosive," I whispered to Will, and grabbed the breaching charge off the back of my kit.

We both knew that time was of the essence and the element of surprise was gone the minute our helicopter crashed. Will set the sledgehammer aside and covered the door with his rifle.

From across the compound, there was an explosion as the team from Chalk Two blew the north gate open. "Failed breach" came over the radio. "We're moving to the Delta Compound gate at this time." After blowing the gate open, they had discovered a brick wall sealing it. The team was supposed to be assaulting the third floor by now, but they were still trying to gain entry.

"Roger, I will meet you there and unlock it from the inside," Mike replied.

Delta gate was at the north end of the driveway that separated the helicopter crash with the rest of the compound. Mike was on the south end of the driveway, close to the guest-house.

The mission was moving quickly now. It had probably been about five minutes since we hit the ground, and now twenty-four guys were swarming the compound. At least two charges had blown and, coupled with the helicopters, we knew they had heard us coming. Without a doubt, we figured the occupants of the compound would now be prepared to defend themselves.

Taking a knee to the right of the door, I peeled the backing off the adhesive strip on the breaching charge and set it across the mangled knob and lock. I always knelt while I placed breaching charges because I had been shot at through the door in Iraq many times. Fighters liked to spray the middle of the door, blindly firing where they thought a man would be standing.

The third member of my team entered the compound. He was one of the last guys out of the helicopter and had just gotten to us. His job was to clear a staircase that led to the roof of the guesthouse. As he started toward the stairs, which were directly in line with the door, AK-47 rounds tore through the glass above the door, narrowly missing him.

I rolled away as the bullets cracked just inches over my head. The first rounds always surprise the shit out of you. I could feel pieces of glass hit my shoulder.

"That is not a suppressed weapon," I thought.

It was easy to tell who was firing, since we had suppressors on our weapons. Unsuppressed rounds meant enemy fire. Someone inside had an assault rifle. Aiming chest high, he fired a blind barrage. He was a caged animal. There was nowhere he could go and he knew we were coming.

Will, covering the door from the left side, started to fire back instantly. As I turned back and opened fire, I felt a searing burn in my left shoulder, probably glass or shrapnel. Our return fire cut through the metal door.

Rolling out of the "fatal funnel" of the doorway, I made it to my feet and moved to the window a few feet down the wall from the door.

"Ahmed al-Kuwaiti," Will said. "Ahmed al-Kuwaiti, come out!"

Smashing the window with my barrel, I fired back toward his likely position.

Will was still yelling, and with no response. With no time to spare, I made my way back to the explosive charge, which was still hanging from the door. The only way to get inside was to blow the door. As I got close, I made sure to stay extra low.

Once we blew the door, I planned to throw a grenade inside before we went in to clear it. Ahmed al-Kuwaiti had proven he wasn't going down without a fight, and I was not going to risk anything.

I was about to attach the detonator to the charge when we heard someone throwing the latch to the lock. Will heard it too, and we both immediately started to back away from the door. We had no idea who was coming out or what to expect.

Was he going to just crack the door and throw a grenade, or hang his AK-47 out and spray?

I took a quick look around. There was no cover. The courtyard was crowded with trash and tools used to garden. Our only option was to continue moving back, trying to stay away from the window and door.

The door cracked open slowly, and I could hear a woman's voice calling out. That didn't mean we were safe. If she was coming out with a suicide vest on, we were dead. This was Bin Laden's compound. These were his facilitators. Shots were fired, so we knew they were willing to die to protect him.

Through the sweat running down my face and the grit in my eyes from the rotor wash, I could just make out the figure of a woman in the green glow of my night vision goggles. She had something in her arms and my finger slowly started applying pressure to my trigger. I could see our lasers dancing around her head. It would only take a split second to end her life if she was holding a bomb.

As the door continued to open, I saw that the bundle was a baby. Al-Kuwaiti's wife, Mariam, came out with the child pressed against her chest. Behind her, three more kids shuffled out of the house.

"Come here," Will called out to her in Arabic.

I kept my rifle trained on them as they moved forward.

"He is dead," Mariam said to Will in Arabic. "You shot him. He is dead. You killed him."

Will did a quick pat down of the woman.

"Hey, she is saying he is dead," Will said to me, translating her Arabic.

I was crouched at the right side of the door and pushed it open.

I spotted a pair of feet lying in the doorway of the bed room. There was no way of knowing if he was still alive, and I wasn't taking any chances. Will gave me a squeeze on the shoulder so I knew he was ready, and we entered the hallway. I shouldered my rifle and squeezed off several rounds to make sure he was down.

The house smelled of heating oil. Stepping over al-Kuwaiti's body, I saw a pistol and an AK-47 on the ground just inside the bedroom door. I kicked them away and continued to clear the room, which had a bed in the center and then smaller beds along the walls for the children. The whole family slept in the same room.

On the other side of the hall was a kitchen area. Our return fire had destroyed the room, shredding the pantry and exploding dry goods all over. Water trickled off the counter. The stove had several holes in it and the cheap tile was smashed, with chunks strewn across the counter and floor.

The floor was slippery from the water and al-Kuwaiti's blood, which had pooled in the hall and gotten on our boots. We hastily cleared both rooms and headed outside.

"Shots fired C1, building is secure at this time," I said over troop net, and tossed an IR chemlight at the guesthouse's front door. We moved toward the main building to backfill the other teams.

CHAPTER 14

Khalid

Not even ten minutes had passed since we crashed. Will and I sprinted through the open gate between the guesthouse and the main compound.

We were headed toward the north door of A1.

"Explosives set, north door A1," Charlie said over the troop net.

His charge was set and he was waiting for the order to blow the north door. All Charlie and Walt needed now was the radio call from Tom to initiate.

Jen and her analysts were right so far. They suspected that the house was split into a duplex. The Bin Laden family lived on the second and third floors with their own private entrance.

The Pacer always came out the north door but the al-Kuwaiti brothers always used the south door.

Unsure if a hallway ran between the north and south doors, we didn't want to risk two explosive breaches at the same time. So Tom and his team had come up with a plan to clear the south side of the house first, while Charlie waited for Tom's radio call before setting off the explosive charge.

Tom's three-man team was inside clearing the first floor. Inside the building was dark, almost pitch-black, but under night vision they could easily make out the hallway and four doors opening off the long hall, two on each side. Tom's team was no more than a few steps inside the house when the point man spotted a man's head sticking out of the first room on the left. They had already heard the unmistakable sound of AK-47 fire coming from the guesthouse, and they weren't taking any chances. There was ample time for whoever was in A1 to get ready to put up a fight.

The point man snapped off a shot. The round struck the occupant, later confirmed to be Abrar al-Kuwaiti, and he disappeared into the room. Slowly moving down the hall, the team stopped at the door. Abrar al-Kuwaiti was wounded and struggling on the floor. Just as they opened fire again, his wife Bushra jumped in the way to shield him. The second burst of rounds killed both of them.

The team saw another woman and several children huddled in the corner crying. An AK-47 was in the room. Grabbing the rifle, Tom unloaded it while the rest of the team searched the remaining rooms.

At the end of the hall was a locked door, which was directly in line with the north door. With the south side of A1 secure, Tom's team quickly exited.

Usually, we would have left someone to watch the woman and kids in the bedroom, but we didn't have the time or enough assaulters. The remaining woman and kids were just left in the room.

"Hey, Charlie, send it," Tom said on the troop net.

As they exited the south door, one of the SEALs threw Abrar al-Kuwaiti's AK-47 into the courtyard. It was dark and there was little chance anyone would come out looking for it.

Seconds after hearing the call from Tom over the radio, I heard the boom as Charlie set off his breaching charge. Will and I had made our way around the west side of the building and stacked behind the guys lined up to enter the north door, which was now open.

The SEALs from Chalk Two had by now made their way into the compound. After the failed breach, they had moved over to the main gate and were let in by Mike. They were already stacked on the north door.

Charlie was already inside, and a loose line had formed as the rest of us waited to enter the target. Through my night vision I could see multiple lasers tracking along the windows and balconies just in case. Scanning my laser above me toward the second and third floor, I didn't see any movement. Coating on the windows made it impossible to see in or out.

All of the rushing around had begun to slow. Things were going very smoothly since the crash ten minutes ago. We all wanted to continue the assault up the stairs, but Charlie reported over the radio that an additional metal gate was blocking our path to the second floor. Charlie was busy setting his third explosive charge of the night.

All we could do was wait and pull security. I knew Charlie and the others were working as fast as they possibly could. While I was standing there I began to think about how surreal it all was. It felt like waiting to start a CQB run during Green Team.

The sound of some pissed-off chickens pulled me from my thoughts. Our route to the north door had taken us through a small area of latticework and chicken coops. Our bulletproof vests and tactical gear were getting hung up in the narrow walkway, smashing the coops.

Standing in one place was driving me crazy.

Just in front of me I could hear a couple of guys talking.

"Holy shit, I can't believe we just crashed," Walt said.

"Crashed, what the fuck are you talking about?"

"Yeah, our helo just crashed," Walt said.

Standing nearby was Jay, the mission's commander, who had been on Chalk Two. When he heard Walt talk about the crash, he quickly cut in.

"What?"

"Yeah, we crashed," Walt said, motioning back toward the crash site. "You might want to take a look in the courtyard."

Even through night vision I thought it looked funny as the expression on Jay's face changed as he processed the information. He turned and sprinted back down the line of assaulters. I guess no one from Chalk Two knew we crashed. At this point, it had not been broadcast over the net. When the pilots of Chalk Two saw Chalk One go down in the courtyard, they had skipped the risky fast-rope onto the roof, and landed Chalk Two outside the walls.

Back at the helicopter, Teddy and his crew were shutting down the engines and making sure all of the instruments were destroyed. For a second, he considered attempting to take off again. There was no major visible damage to the helicopter, and he figured with no weight he might be able to lift off. In the end, caution won out.

After rushing to the scene of the crash, Jay immediately got on the satellite radio he was carrying and called the QRF.

The QRF quickly took off from their initial position, located with the second CH-47 a short distance north of the compound, and headed our way. To save time, they took the most direct route over Pakistan's military academy. But a few minutes later, Jay called back. Although we had crash-landed, we didn't have any dead or wounded. All the assaulters were consolidated on A1 and they were about to start clearing up the stairs.

"Hold your position," he said to the QRF.

Inside A1, Charlie set his next breaching charge and checked the back blast. Since the charge was going to explode inside the building, the over pressure was more dynamic and would blow out windows and doors. Two other SEALs were near Charlie. With almost zero cover to shield them from the blast, one SEAL was hiding behind a door that led to another room.

"Hey, buddy, you might want to watch out for that door," Charlie said.

The assaulter stepped away from behind the door just as Charlie set off the charge. I could hear the loud boom echo from my position outside at the chicken coops. The over pressure blew the door the SEAL had been hiding behind from its hinges and sent it crashing into the opposite wall. The SEAL stood there stunned. A few seconds ago, he was in the path and would have likely been seriously injured if he hadn't moved.

"Thanks," he said to Charlie, as they both pushed and pulled open the mangled gate.

With the gate open, we started clearing up the stairs. It took a few seconds for me to get to the door. I hooked right through the second metal gate and began heading up the stairs. Most of the guys were already ahead of me.

The tile stairs were set at ninety-degree angles, creating a sort of spiral staircase separated by small landings. We had no idea what to expect. By now, Bin Laden or whoever was hiding inside had plenty of time to get a weapon and prepare a defense. Since the only way up was through a spiraling staircase, we could easily get bottlenecked.

It was dark and we were doing our best to be quiet. Every step was deliberate.

No talking.

No yelling.

No running.

In the old days, we'd storm the castle, throwing flash grenades as we cleared through an objective. Now we stayed as quiet as possible. We had the advantage with our night vision, but it would be lost if you went barreling into a room. It was all about throttle control. There was no reason to run to our deaths.

When I reached the landing on the second deck, most of the other assaulters had fanned out. The second floor opened into a long hallway heading to a terrace that ran along the south side of the building. The floor had four doors, two right near the landing and two farther down near the terrace. I could see my teammates creeping down the hall, stacking on the doors before quietly clearing inside.

I noticed another assaulter three or four steps up the stairs holding security on the landing between the second and third decks. A body was on the landing. Blood was trickling out onto the marble floor.

While holding security, the assaulter had seen a man quickly poke his head down around the landing. Intelligence reports said there could be up to four males living at the compound. Khalid, one of Bin Laden's sons, was most likely living on the second floor, while Bin Laden lived on the third floor.

The head peeking around the corner was clean-cut with no beard. It had to be Bin Laden's son.

"Khalid," the assaulter whispered. "Khalid."

Everyone in the compound had heard the helicopter engines. They heard the shots fired at the guesthouse, and they heard the explosive breaches.

But by then everything was quiet again. All they could

hear was our footsteps. Then the man on the landing heard his name being called.

They know my name? I imagine him thinking.

Curiosity got the best of him and he stuck his head out to see who was calling his name. The second he stuck his head back around the corner, the assaulter shot him in the face. His body rolled down the stairs and rested on the landing.

Looking back, I saw we had several more SEALs coming up the stairs and beginning to stack behind me. The second-floor hallway was already full of assaulters and they didn't need any more help.

The only place to go was up.

Standing behind the point man, I gave him a squeeze to let him know we were ready.

"Take it."

CHAPTER 15

Third Deck

Khalid was splayed out on his back, and we had to carefully pick our way past him on the stairs.

The steps were slick tile, made slicker by the blood. Each step was precarious. Nearby, I saw Khalid's AK-47 rifle propped on the step.

"I am glad he didn't man up and use that thing," I thought.

Had the point man not called his name, we could have been pinned down on the stairwell. All he had to do was sit on the landing and fire a few rounds each time we tried to move up the stairs toward his position. That would have been a nightmare, and we would have taken some casualties for sure.

We had planned for more of a fight. For all the talk about

suicide vests and being willing to shed blood for Allah, only one of the al-Kuwaiti brothers got off a barrage. At least Khalid had thought about it. When we examined his AK-47 later, we learned he had a round in the chamber. He was prepared to fight, but in the end, he hadn't gotten much of an opportunity.

The stairwell was pitch-black to the naked eye, but under our night vision everything was bathed in a green hue. The assaulter holding security was now on point as we followed him up the stairs. We were again slowing down and taking our time. The point man was the eyes and ears for the rest of us. He controlled the pace.

Throttle on. Throttle off.

So far, everything was adding up. We knew the house had at least four men. The only one left was Bin Laden. But I pushed those thoughts out of my head. It didn't matter who it was on the third deck. We were possibly walking into a gunfight, and most gunfights at this range only last a few seconds. There was no margin of error.

"Focus," I told myself.

With the point man directly in front of me, there was nothing much I could do. I was there to support him. Roughly fifteen minutes had passed and Bin Laden had plenty of time to strap on a suicide vest or simply get his gun.

My eyes scanned the landing up ahead. My senses were on overdrive. My ears strained to hear a round being chambered or the footsteps of someone approaching. Nothing we were doing was new. We had all been on hundreds of missions. At the most basic level, we were clearing rooms like we learned in

Green Team. Only the target and the fact that we were in Pakistan made this mission significant.

The landing at the top of the stairs opened into a narrow hallway. At the end of the hall was a door to the balcony. Roughly five feet from the top of the stairs were two doors, one to the right and one to the left.

The stairway was relatively narrow, especially for a bunch of guys in kit. It was difficult to see around the point man, since the stairwell and landing narrowed as we got to the top.

We were less than five steps from getting to the top when I heard suppressed shots.

BOP. BOP.

The point man had seen a man peeking out of the door on the right side of the hallway about ten feet in front of him. I couldn't tell from my position if the rounds hit the target or not. The man disappeared into the dark room.

The point man reached the landing first and slowly moved toward the door. Unlike in the movies, we didn't bound up the final few steps and rush into the room with guns blazing. We took our time.

The point man kept his rifle trained into the room as we slowly crept toward the open door. Again, we didn't rush. Instead, we waited at the threshold and peered inside. We could see two women standing over a man lying at the foot of a bed. Both women were dressed in long gowns and their hair was a tangled mess like they had been sleeping. The women were hysterically crying and wailing in Arabic. The younger one looked up and saw us at the door.

She yelled out in Arabic and rushed the point man. We were less than five feet apart. Swinging his gun to the side, the point man grabbed both women and drove them toward the corner of the room. If either woman had on a suicide vest, he probably saved our lives, but it would have cost him his own. It was a selfless decision made in a split second.

With the women out of the way, I entered the room with a third SEAL. We saw the man lying on the floor at the foot of his bed. He was wearing a white sleeveless T-shirt, loose tan pants, and a tan tunic. The point man's shots had entered the right side of his head. Blood and brains spilled out of the side of his skull. In his death throes, he was still twitching and convulsing. Another assaulter and I trained our lasers on his chest and fired several rounds. The bullets tore into him, slamming his body into the floor until he was motionless.

Quickly scanning for additional threats, I saw at least three children huddled in the far corner of the room near the sliding glass door that opened onto the balcony. The children—I couldn't tell if they were boys or girls—sat in the corner, stunned, as I cleared the room.

With the man on the floor now motionless and no further threat, we cleared two small rooms just off the bedroom. Pushing the first door open, I peeked inside and saw a small, cramped, messy office. Papers were strewn all over a tiny desk. The second door revealed a small shower and toilet.

Everything was muscle memory now. In our minds, we started ticking off our mental checklist. The main threat was dead by the bed. The point man was covering the women and kids. My teammate and I cleared the small office and bath-room, while the other SEALs cleared the room across the hall.

As I went across the hall to the other room, I passed Walt on the way.

"All clear over here," he said.

"This side too," I replied.

The point man moved the women and kids out of the bedroom and onto the balcony to keep them calm. Tom was on the third deck and saw that both rooms were clear.

"Third deck secure," I heard him say over the troop net.

CHAPTER 16

Geronimo

Back in the bedroom, the youngest woman was lying on the bed, screaming hysterically, clutching her calf.

Walt was standing next to the body. It was still dark and it was hard to make out the man's face. The house was still without power. I reached up and flipped on the light clipped into the rail system on my helmet. The target was now secure and since all the windows were covered, no one could see us from the outside, so the use of white light was safe.

The man's face was mangled from at least one bullet wound and covered in blood. A hole in his forehead collapsed the right side of his skull. His chest was torn up from where the bullets had entered his body. He was lying in an ever-growing pool of blood. As I crouched down to take a closer look, Tom joined me.

"I think this is our boy," Tom said.

He wasn't about to say it was Bin Laden over the radio because he knew that call would be shot like lightning back to Washington. We knew President Obama was listening, so we didn't want to be wrong.

I went through the checklist in my head.

He was very tall. I figured approximately six foot four inches.

Check.

He was the one adult male on the third deck.

Check.

The two couriers were exactly where the CIA said they'd be.

Check.

The more I looked at his mangled face, my eye seemed to go back to his nose. It wasn't damaged and seemed familiar. Pulling my booklet out of my kit, I studied the composite photos. The long and slender nose fit. His beard was dark black and there was no trace of the gray that I expected to see.

"Walt and I will run with this," I said to Tom.

"Roger," Tom said.

Taking out my camera and rubber gloves, I started taking photos while Walt prepared to take multiple sets of DNA samples.

Will, the Arabic speaker, was in the room treating the leg wound of the woman crying on the bed. We learned later that she was Amal al-Fatah, Bin Laden's fifth wife. I'm not sure

Operation Neptune Spear   (May 1, 2011)

The plan called for two Black Hawk helicopters to ferry twenty-two SEALs, an EOD tech, and a CIA interpreter from a base in Jalalabad, Afghanistan, to the target compound located in Abbottabad, Pakistan. Two CH-47s that carried extra fuel and a quick reaction force of additional SEALs set up a forward refueling point fifteen minutes from the target.

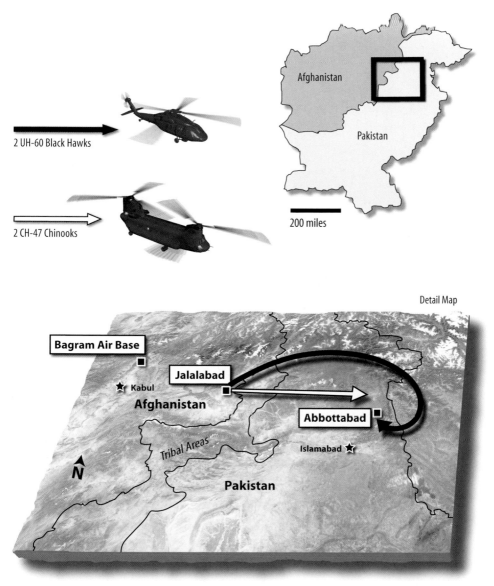

2 UH-60 Black Hawks

2 CH-47 Chinooks

Afghanistan

Pakistan

200 miles

Detail Map

Bagram Air Base

Jalalabad

Kabul

Afghanistan

Abbottabad

Tribal Areas

Islamabad

N

Pakistan

50 miles

Osama bin Laden's Compound

The one-acre compound was on Kakul Road in Bilal Town, a middle-class neighborhood in the city of Abbottabad. The town is home to a Pakistani military academy and a popular vacation spot. Bin Laden lived in the main house on the third floor.

*Walls surrounding compound were topped with barbed wire

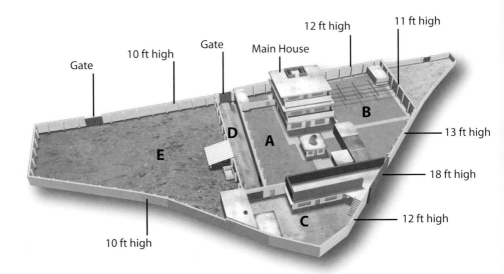

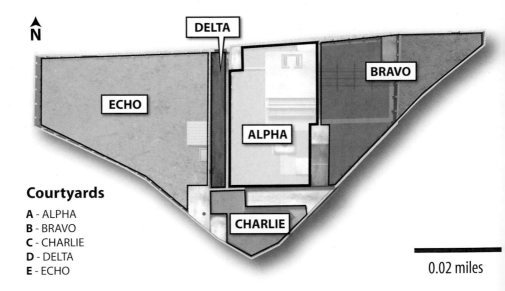

Courtyards

A - ALPHA
B - BRAVO
C - CHARLIE
D - DELTA
E - ECHO

0.02 miles

Operation Neptune Spear: Infil

① Chalk One attempted to hover over "A" courtyard but was unable to hold station and crash landed.

② Chalk Two landed and inserted the external security team consisting of four SEALs, an interpreter, and the combat assault dog.

③ The pilots flying Chalk One were able to crash the helicopter in "E" courtyard, west of the main house.

④ Chalk Two saw Chalk One crashing, and the pilot immediately made the safer decision of landing outside the gate instead of attempting the fast rope insert onto the top of the main building.

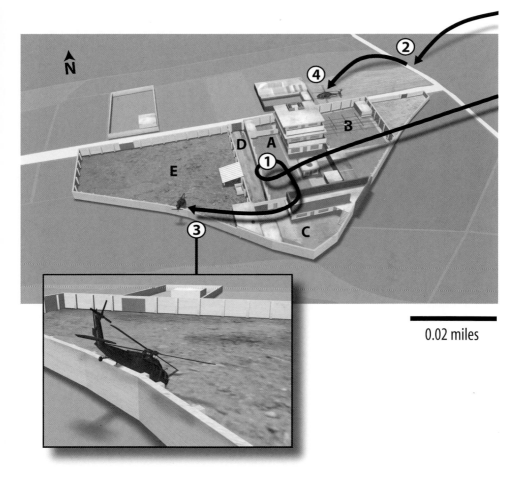

0.02 miles

Operation Neptune Spear: Assault

After Chalk One crashed, the SEALs quickly recovered and began the assault.

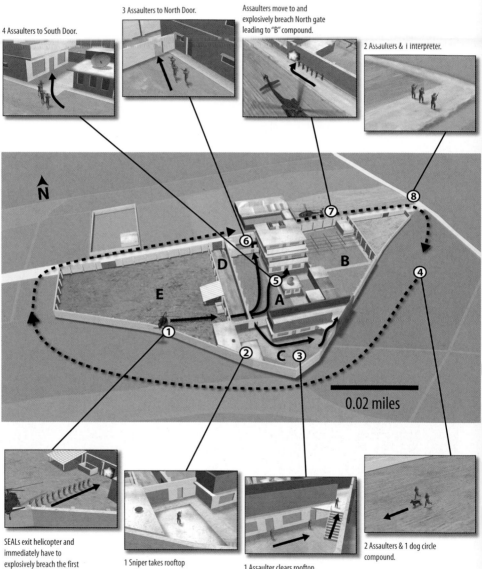

4 Assaulters to South Door.

3 Assaulters to North Door.

Assaulters move to and explosively breach North gate leading to "B" compound.

2 Assaulters & 1 Interpreter.

N

D

E

A

B

C

6

5

1

2

3

4

7

8

0.02 miles

SEALs exit helicopter and immediately have to explosively breach the first gate.

1 Sniper takes rooftop position.

1 Assaulter clears rooftop.
2 Assaulters clear building.

2 Assaulters & 1 dog circle compound.

Operation Neptune Spear: The Main House

① Chalk Two breached the gate with explosives only to find it blocked by a brick wall. Chalk Two moved to and enters the "D" gate.

② Mike, the senior enlisted SEAL on the mission, let Chalk Two in at the compound's "D" or main gate.

③ After clearing "C" compound, Owen's team headed to the main house to assist in the assault

④ Blocked by a metal gate in the hallway, Tom and his team clear the Southern portion of the first floor and then exit and head to the North door.

⑤ Charlie places an explosive charge on the North door and waits for the call from Tom before initiating the charge.

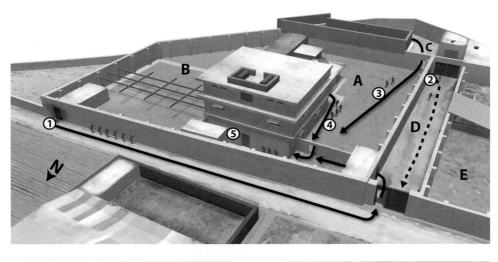

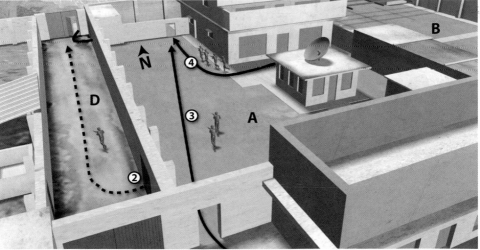

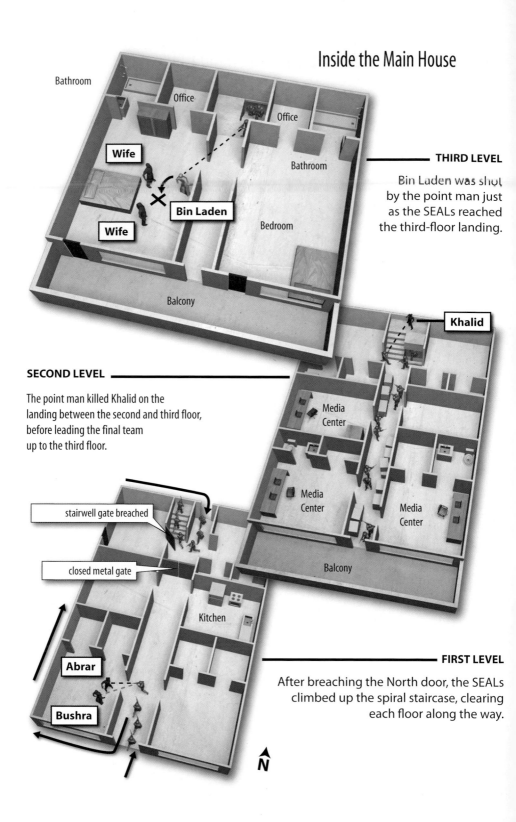

Inside the Main House

THIRD LEVEL

Bin Laden was shot by the point man just as the SEALs reached the third-floor landing.

Bathroom

Office

Office

Wife

Bathroom

Bin Laden

Bedroom

Wife

Balcony

Khalid

SECOND LEVEL

The point man killed Khalid on the landing between the second and third floor, before leading the final team up to the third floor.

Media Center

Media Center

Media Center

Balcony

stairwell gate breached

closed metal gate

Kitchen

FIRST LEVEL

After breaching the North door, the SEALs climbed up the spiral staircase, clearing each floor along the way.

Abrar

Bushra

N

Operation Neptune Spear: Exfil

1. The SEALs move Bin Laden's body out of the compound.

2. Chalk One moves through the field and boards the Black Hawk helicopter.

3. With only seconds to spare the CH-47 was told to conduct an immediate go-around to the South to avoid flying debris from the explosive charges set on the downed Black Hawk.

4. Helicopter explodes.

5. Chalk Two and the downed Black Hawk helicopter crew board the CH-47 carrying the quick reaction force.

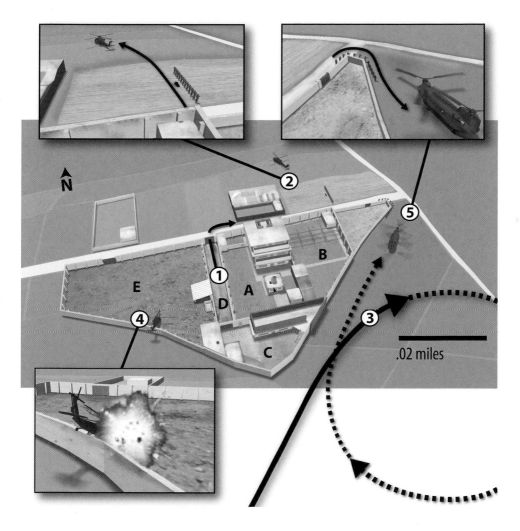

Operation Neptune Spear: Exfil

(1) One CH-47 picks up the SEALs at the compound and flies direclty back to Jalalabad.

(2) Black Hawk flies north, landing at the FARP (Forward Air Refueling Point) site.

(3) Black Hawk and CH-47 fly directly back to Jalalabad.

(4) C-130 flies assault element from Jalalabad to Bagram.

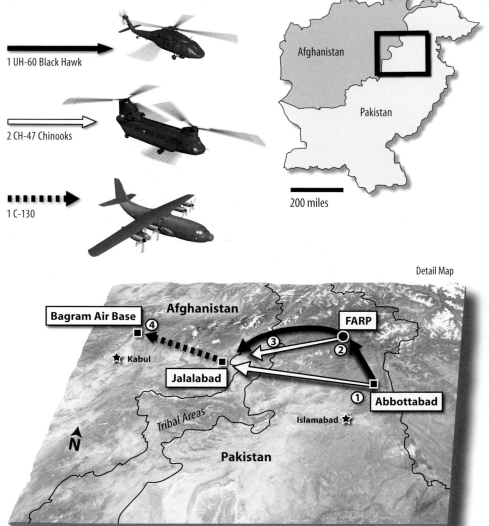

1 UH-60 Black Hawk

2 CH-47 Chinooks

1 C-130

Afghanistan

Pakistan

200 miles

Detail Map

50 miles

when she got hit, but it was a very small wound. It could have been from bullet fragments or a ricochet.

"Hey, we have a significant amount of SSE on the second deck," I heard someone call over the troop net. "We're going to need any extra bodies down here."

As Tom left the room, I heard him on the command net.

"We have a possible, I repeat POSSIBLE touchdown on the third deck."

Walt pulled his CamelBak hose from his kit and squirted water on the man's face.

I started to wipe the blood away from his face using a blanket from the bed. With each swipe, the face became more familiar. He looked younger than I expected. His beard was dark, like it had been dyed. I just kept thinking about how he didn't look anything like I'd expected him to look.

It was strange to see such an infamous face up close. Lying in front of me was the reason we had been fighting for the last decade. It was surreal trying to clean blood off the most wanted man in the world so that I could shoot his photo. I had to focus on the mission. Right now, we needed some good quality photos. This picture could end up being widely viewed, and I didn't want to mess it up.

Tossing the blanket away, I pulled out the camera that I'd used to shoot hundreds of pictures over the last few years and started snapping photos. We'd all gotten real good taking these kinds of photos. We'd been playing CSI Afghanistan for years.

The first shots were of his full body. Then I knelt down near his head and shot a few of just his face. Pulling his beard to the right and then the left, I shot several profile pictures. I really wanted to focus on the nose. Because the beard was so dark, the profile shot was the one that really stood out in my mind.

"Hey, man, hold his good eye open," I said to Walt.

He reached down and peeled back the eyelid, exposing his now lifeless brown eye. I zoomed in and shot a tight photo of it. While I shot pictures, Will was with the women and children on the balcony. Below us, my teammates were collecting all of the computers, memory cards, notebooks, and videos. Outside, Ali, the CIA interpreter, and the security team were dealing with curious neighbors.

Over the radio, I heard Mike talking about the crashed Black Hawk.

"Demo team, prep it to blow," Mike said.

I knew from the radio traffic that the SEAL in charge of demolition and the EOD tech were on their way to the courtyard.

"Hey, we're going to blow it," the SEAL said.

"Roger that," the EOD tech said. He started taking out charges and putting them around the ground floor of the main house.

"What the fuck?" the SEAL said as the EOD tech unpacked.

Everybody was confused.

"You told me to get ready to blow it, right?"

"Not the house," the SEAL said. "The helo."

"What helo?"

The EOD tech thought the SEAL meant they were going

to blow the house, which was another one of the contingency plans we had trained for.

News of Chalk One's crash was still not widespread. People were just finding out about it. In Washington, they weren't even sure we'd crashed when they watched it on the drone feed. I heard later it looked on the grainy black-and-white video as if we'd "parked" in the courtyard and let the team out. The president and senior staff were confused when it happened, and even asked JSOC what was going on. A quick message to McRaven came back with an answer: "We will now be amending the mission . . . we have a helicopter down in the courtyard. My men are prepared for this contingency, and they will deal with it."

Outside, the helicopter crew was done destroying all of the classified gear. Teddy, the senior pilot and flight lead, was one of the last to climb out. Getting to the door, he looked at the almost six-foot drop to the ground. There was no way he wanted to jump and risk injury. Kicking the fast rope out of the cabin, he slid down to the courtyard, which made him the only guy to fast-rope into the compound that night.

The EOD tech and the SEAL got there soon after and started to place explosive charges around the fuselage. Climbing up the tail, the SEAL tried to get charges as close to the tail rotors as possible. Wearing his kit and night vision goggles wasn't the easiest way to climb up the unstable, narrow section of tail boom. Each time he tried to reach the section propped on the twelve-foot wall, he was afraid it would break under his weight.

Climbing up as high as he could, he placed the charges with one hand. The other hand kept him stable as he balanced precariously over the courtyard. Destroying the communications equipment and avionics was the most important part. With the charges set on the tail, he placed the remaining charges in the main cabin.

Meanwhile, the Black Hawk that hadn't crashed and the CH-47 carrying the QRF were flying in circles nearby, waiting for us to finish. Fuel was becoming an issue, which meant our time in the compound was shrinking quickly.

"Ten minutes," I heard Mike say over the radio.

On the third deck, the lights in the room came on, bathing us in the glow of white light. The rolling blackout was apparently over. It was perfect timing and made everything easier.

While I continued shooting pictures, Walt took DNA samples. He dabbed a cotton swab in Bin Laden's blood. He took another and jammed it in Bin Laden's mouth to get a saliva sample. Finally, he took out a spring-loaded syringe the CIA gave us to get a blood-marrow sample. We'd been trained to jab it into the thigh to get a sample from inside the femur. Walt jabbed it several times into Bin Laden's thigh, but the needle wouldn't fire.

"Here," I said, handing him mine. "Try this one."

He took it and slammed my syringe into the fleshy part of Bin Laden's thigh, but it also didn't fire.

"Fuck these things," Walt said, tossing the syringes to the side.

I finished taking a second set of pictures using another

SEAL's camera. We took two DNA samples and sets of photos so that we had identical sets. Walt put one sample in his cargo pocket and gave another to a SEAL in the other chalk. This had been carefully planned so if one of the helicopters was shot down on our flight back to Jalalabad, a DNA sample and set of pictures would survive. We wanted proof to show to Pakistan and the rest of the world we got Bin Laden.

Meanwhile, on the balcony, Will was trying to get confirmation that it was Bin Laden on the floor.

Bin Laden's wife Amal, who had been wounded in the ankle, was still hysterical and wouldn't talk. I could hear her whimpering on the bed above me while I worked. The other woman, her eyes puffy from crying, tried to keep a stern face as Will asked her over and over again in Arabic who the dead guy was.

"What is his name?"

"The sheikh," the woman said.

"The sheikh who?" Will said. He didn't want to lead her and stuck to open-ended questions.

After she gave Will several aliases, he went over to the kids who were outside on the balcony. They were all sitting silently against the wall. Will knelt down and asked one of the girls, "Who is the man?"

The girl didn't know to lie.

"Osama bin Laden."

Will smiled.

"Are you sure that is Osama bin Laden?"

"Yes," the girl said.

"OK," he said. "Thanks."

Back in the hallway, he grabbed one of the wives by her arms and gave her a good shake.

"Stop fucking with me now," Will said, more sternly than before. "Who is that in the bedroom?"

She started to cry. More scared than anything else, she didn't have any fight left.

"Osama," she said.

"Osama what?" Will said, still holding her arm.

"Osama bin Laden," she said.

Will moved her back outside with the kids and walked back into the bedroom.

"Hey, dual confirmation," Will said. "Confirmed it with the kid. Confirmed it with the old lady. Both are saying the same thing."

As Will left the room, Jay showed up with Tom. Seeing the body, he came and stood over it.

"Will confirmed through a woman and a kid that it is UBL," Tom said.

Kneeling next to his head, I pulled his beard to the left and right so Jay could get the profile shot. I had my SSE card and put it next to his face so Jay could see the real Bin Laden next to the CIA renderings.

"Yeah, that looks like our guy," Jay said.

Jay immediately left the room to call it in. The rest of us went back to work. Once outside, Jay got on the satellite radio to Admiral McRaven, who was still in Jalalabad. The admiral was keeping President Obama and the rest of the situation room in the White House updated on our progress.

"For God and country, I pass Geronimo," Jay said. "Geronimo E.K.I.A."

Over the troop net I could hear the guys on the second deck. They needed more help to gather up all of the intelligence in the media rooms. It was on the second floor that Bin Laden had a makeshift office where he kept his computers and made his video pronouncements.

The rooms were immaculate and organized. Everything had its place. All of his CDs, DVDs, and memory cards were stacked up perfectly. The SEALs focused on grabbing all the electronic media—recorders, memory cards, thumb drives, and computers. The CIA had briefed us on what type of digital voice recorder they thought Bin Laden used and had even showed us one that was similar during our training. The SEALs searching the second floor actually found one exactly like the CIA had predicted. I marveled again at the intelligence team. When Jen had pronounced one hundred percent, I should have believed her.

When we were done with the DNA samples and photos, Walt and another SEAL grabbed Bin Laden's legs and pulled him out of the room. With all the commotion and activity going on around me, I can still remember watching the guys drag his body down the stairs.

I stayed in the room and started gathering up any intelligence I could find. The office was barren of anything useful. I grabbed a few papers, possibly religious writings, and took some audiocassettes and threw them into a mesh bag. We all carried the lightweight, collapsible bags for this purpose. A quick search of the tiny bathroom with green tile on the walls had revealed nothing of value. I did find a box of Just For Men hair dye, which he must have used on his beard. No wonder he looked so young when we found him.

On the wall between the bathroom and office, I opened up a wooden freestanding dresser. It was about six feet tall with two long doors. Inside were several sets of clothes, including the long shirts, baggy pants, and vests common to the region.

I was shocked by how neat it was. Compared to some parts of his house, which looked like hoarders lived there, his dresser could have passed a Marine Corps Boot Camp inspection. All of his T-shirts were folded into squares and stacked in one corner. His clothes hung evenly spaced.

"This could be my dresser," I thought.

I grabbed a few shirts and a vest and stuffed them in my bag. I knew we were there to collect mostly electronic media, but since there wasn't much of that in the room I figured I'd grab this stuff instead. Throwing open the drawers at the bottom, I rifled through his stuff, looking for anything useful. For the most part, his room appeared to be for sleeping.

Before I left, I noticed a shelf that ran above the door. It was just above where he was standing when we got to the third deck. I slid my hand up and felt two guns, which turned out to be an AK-47 and a Makarov pistol in a holster. I took each weapon down and pulled out the magazine and checked the chambers.

They were both empty.

He hadn't even prepared a defense. He had no intention of fighting. He asked his followers for decades to wear suicide vests or fly planes into buildings, but didn't even pick up his weapon. In all of my deployments, we routinely saw this phenomenon. The higher up the food chain the targeted individual was, the bigger a pussy he was. The leaders were less willing to fight. It is always the young and impressionable who strap on the explosives and blow themselves up.

Bin Laden knew we were coming when he heard the helicopter. I had more respect for Ahmed al-Kuwaiti in the guesthouse because at least he tried to defend himself and his family. Bin Laden had more time to prepare than the others, and yet he still didn't do anything. Did he believe his own message? Was he willing to fight the war he asked for? I don't think so. Otherwise, he would have at least gotten his gun and stood up for what he believed. There is no honor in sending people to die for something you won't even fight for yourself.

Over the radio, I could hear updates from the team on the security perimeter.

Ali and the four SEALs spent most of our time on target holding security along the road northeast of the compound. After they were inserted, two assaulters and Cairo, the combat assault dog, did a sweep of the perimeter.

After the patrol, they waited and watched for onlookers to

come out and investigate the commotion. Residents heard the helicopters, the intermittent explosions, and gunfire. Wondering what was going on, a few small groups approached the security team.

"Go back inside," Ali said in Pashto. "There is a security operation under way."

Luckily for us, the Pakistanis obliged and went back into their houses. A few posted messages on Twitter about helicopters and noise.

Time was getting tight.

Mike was on the radio giving us remaining-time hacks. We'd been in the compound for almost thirty minutes. Each time he came on, my teammates on the second deck asked for additional time.

"We need ten more minutes," a SEAL on the second deck said. "We're not even halfway done."

Mike just repeated the time back calmly. The mission was a balancing act. We all wanted to stay and make sure we didn't leave anything behind, but the helicopters were running out of fuel and there wasn't any time to give.

"Post assault, five minutes," Mike finally said. That meant drop what you're doing and get to the landing zone within five minutes.

I was done on the third deck, and I started for the door. I felt like I was leaving something undone. We took pride in coming back with every bit of intelligence we could find and collect. There was so much still to do. We all had to face the fact we were leaving areas unsearched, and then put it out of our minds. We all knew the risks of running out of gas or remaining on target too long, giving the local police or military time to react. We got what we came for: Bin Laden. It was time to get out while we still could.

"Hey, consolidate the women and children and get them out of the compound," Mike said over the radio.

I could hear Will trying to get the women and children to move outside. We didn't want them to wander over to the helicopter before it exploded. But it was like herding cats, and Will wasn't making any headway. The women were still sobbing, and the kids were either crying or sitting in a daze. None of them wanted to move.

I didn't have time to help. I still needed to get over to C compound. I followed the smear of blood from Bin Laden's body. It left a slippery trail all the way to the first deck, where Walt had put Bin Laden's body into a body bag. As I climbed down the steps, I could see where they'd dragged the body over Khalid's body. His son's white shirt was stained with his father's blood.

I headed for C1. The others had gotten photos and DNA of al-Kuwaiti. When I got there, his wife and kids were squatting in the corner of the courtyard. I tried to get them up and moving when Mike's urgent call came across the radio.

"Hey, guys," he said. "Drop what you're doing and move to exfil HLZ."

Low on fuel, the Black Hawk and the C-47 were inbound to pick us up. Using arm signals, I got al-Kuwaiti's family up and shepherded them into the guesthouse. I knew the charges on the helicopter were going off nearby. This was going to be a big explosion, but the guesthouse was far enough away. They'd be safe if they stayed inside the room.

Once inside, I tried to get across the idea that there was going to be a big explosion, using my hands and making an explosion sound.

"Stay here," I said in English.

I have no idea if they understood. I backed out of the room and shut the door behind me.

Racing down the rutted driveway, I saw Teddy and the other helicopter crew standing near Mike. They looked funny in their large aviation helmets and Army ACU uniforms. They looked lost and out of their environment, uncomfortable with actually being on the ground.

I looked at Mike as I passed.

"The women and kids are staying in C1," I said. "There is no way I can move them."

The SEALs from the second deck were spilling out of the building. We looked like a gypsy camp, or like Santa Claus on Christmas Eve. Guys had mesh bags over their shoulders so full they seemed to waddle more than run. I saw one SEAL carrying a CPU in one hand and a leather gym bag overflowing in the other. The SEALs on the second floor had collected so much intelligence material that they had run out of the collapsible bags that they carried and started taking bags that they found in the house and filling them too. SEALs carried 1950s leather briefcases like they were on their way to the office, and knockoff Adidas athletic bags as if heading home from the gym.

Outside the gate I turned right and sprinted toward the rest of the guys who were beginning to line up in our chalk loads. I could see the snipers had already set up the landing zone. My chalk was going to exfil on the remaining Black Hawk because we had the body. The smaller, more maneuverable aircraft had less of a chance of being shot down. The CH-47 would pick up all the SEALs from Chalk Two as well as Teddy and his crew from the crashed Black Hawk.

All around us, lights in the houses were on. I could see several heads in the windows watching us. Ali was barking in Pashtu for them to go back inside. We started to get a head count. I was missing Will.

"Where's Will?" I said, moving down the line.

"He was getting the kids and women when I left," Walt said, standing next to the body, ready to move it to the helicopter.

I started to get on the radio to try and find his location when I saw Will run out of the compound. He was the last one out.

Taking my place near Walt on the body bag, I could make out the Black Hawk coming in right on top of the IR strobe in the field. As the helicopter flared out, I looked down, shielding my eyes from the cloud of dust and debris from the rotors. Once the cloud passed, we picked up the body and took off on a dead sprint toward the waiting helicopter. This was our freedom bird and we weren't going to miss it.

The field was recently plowed and we stumbled over eighteen-inch mounds of earth as we hustled the one hundred yards to the helicopter, carrying the six-foot-four body. We looked like drunks stumbling and falling our way to the bird.

The dead weight wasn't easy to carry for any of us, but Walt had a tough time trying to stay upright. Being five foot six inches tall, his stride was much shorter than the rest of us.

Every few steps, he'd fall over one of the mounds. With curse words cascading from his lips, he'd bounce back up and press on.

Racing under the spinning rotors, we threw the body on the deck and quickly climbed aboard. I found a spot up against the back of the pilots' seats. After the sprint, we were exhausted. My chest was heaving, trying to gulp in air.

"Holy shit, we're going to pull this off," I thought.

When we didn't immediately leap into the sky, I got anxious. In Afghanistan, the helicopter was practically taking off with the last boot still on the ground. The longer we waited, the more I prepared for a rocket-propelled grenade to tear through the door.

"Go, go, go," I kept thinking. "Come on man, go. GO!"

But the Black Hawk waited. It even throttled back. The pilots didn't want to take off before the CH-47 arrived. Helicopters liked to fly in pairs. The charges on the downed Black Hawk were seconds away from exploding. The SEAL and EOD tech put the charges on a five-minute timer. That would have been plenty of time if we'd been on schedule.

But we were running late. At this point, we were eight minutes past our planned drop-dead time. We factored in ten extra minutes, but we were about to run out of that too.

We had to assume law enforcement and Pakistani military were inbound and headed to investigate the situation. We were an invading military force who had entered their sovereign territory. I could see the expression on Tom's face. He was on the helicopter's intercom radio trying to figure out what was going on. He wanted the pilots to hurry up and lift off.

"Let's go," he finally said. "We have to take off right now!"

Less than a minute remained on the explosive charges on the downed Black Hawk. The SEAL who set the charges ran up to Jay and grabbed him. They were both still on the landing zone waiting for the CH-47 to arrive. Jay had been so focused on getting the helicopters in safely, he hadn't heard his name being called.

"Call off the 47," the SEAL said to Jay. "You need to get all the birds out of the immediate area, the charge is going to blow in under thirty seconds."

Jay started to work the radios. He knew the explosion would knock the inbound CH-47 out of the sky and shrapnel would destroy the idling Black Hawk.

I heard the rotors come to life, and the Black Hawk quickly climbed into the sky. Swinging to the northeast, we picked up speed. Seconds after takeoff, I saw a big flash of light. The explosion bathed the cabin in light for a second, before it faded back to black.

The CH-47 flew around to the south and landed after the explosion. The remaining SEALs and the aircrew loaded up on the helicopter. Since they'd burned up so much fuel loitering, the CH-47 didn't have any to spare. And with the extra weight of the additional SEALs on board, they had just enough gas to head straight back to the base in Jalalabad.

Closing my eyes, I took a deep breath. The cabin was dark. The only lights were from the dashboard in the cockpit, and from where I was sitting, I could just make out a few gauges on the console, including the gas gauge.

Right when I thought I could relax, I noticed the gas gauge was blinking red. I'm not a pilot, but I knew enough to realize that blinking red lights in a cockpit were never a good sign.

CHAPTER 17

Exfil

I kept peeking into the cockpit to watch the flashing red lights on the gas gauge.

From the briefs leading up to the mission, I remembered it was supposed to take only ten minutes to reach the FARP site. I could feel the helicopter bank and make a wide turn like we were water circling a drain. We seemed to be doing laps around a particular area. The crew chiefs were at the doors scanning the ground from the windows. From the corner of my eye, I could see that the red blinking line on the fuel gauge was even smaller.

Once again, we were jammed into the cabin. Tom was sitting next to me. Walt had to sit on Bin Laden's body, which was lying at my feet in the center of the cabin.

Soon after takeoff, my legs started falling asleep and I tried to wiggle my toes to keep the blood circulating. I knew that in the big scheme of events, our portion of the night's work was now done. Still, none of us could relax until we got fuel and we were safely across the border.

Looking back into the dark cabin again, I forced the fuel issue out of my mind. We were all type A guys who liked to be in control. About thirty-eight minutes ago, all I wanted to do was push the rope out of the helicopter, slide down it, and assault the compound. Now, with that portion of the mission accomplished, I was again stuck in a helicopter with nothing to do.

What good was worrying about fuel going to do? I wasn't a pilot. The red blinking lights could be Christmas lights for all I knew.

The helicopter did another long loop before banking hard and quickly descending into a hover. The crew chief threw open the door and I could finally see the dark silhouette of a CH-47 about fifty yards away.

Some of the SEALs from the other squadron were pulling security in the waist-high grass. As we touched down, they were on one knee facing away from the helicopter, scanning the horizon for signs of the Pakistani military or police. Rotor wash whipped the grass around them.

A pair of Army fuelers wearing goggles to protect their eyes from debris hauled a hose up to the Black Hawk. As the rotors spun, they connected the hose to the fuel tank.

"To save on weight, they want four or five of us to get off

and ride back with the forty-seven," Tom shouted over the noise of the helicopter.

With the additional weight from the body and a full fuel tank, we needed to lighten the load. The pilots were going to err on the side of safety. I saw a couple of guys get off, including Charlie.

Back in Abbottabad, the explosion at the compound had finally attracted the attention of the Pakistani military. Unknown to us, they grounded all of their aircraft and started a head count. With everyone accounted for, they scrambled two F-16 fighters armed with 30mm cannons and air-to-air missiles. Pakistan's military has always maintained a state of high alert against India. Most of the country's air defenses are aimed east toward that threat. The jets roared into the sky and raced toward the Abbottabad area.

Sitting in the helicopter, I checked my watch. I was impatient and wanted to get back to Jalalabad. I wanted to get out and help. We all did, but I knew the fuelers had a job just like we had our job. If I tried to help, it would only slow things down. And right now, the success of the mission hinged on the fuelers getting the helicopter airborne again.

The lone CH-47 that extracted the guys from Chalk Two was long gone when the jets arrived over the compound.

I watched as the fuelers snapped the hoses off our helicopter and dragged them back toward the CH-47. The rotors on their helicopter were starting to spin as the fuelers rolled the hose back up the ramp. The security team peeled back and got on board.

One after the other, both helicopters lifted off and headed west for Afghanistan. No more blinking lights. Now all we needed to do was get back across the border.

I checked my watch again. It took us twenty minutes to refuel. In my mind, I could see Pakistani jets chasing us. I didn't know then, but the F-16s circled around Abbottabad before widening their search.

My brain went back to the booklet on Pakistan's air defenses. There was no chance they didn't know we were there. I just hoped we had a big enough lead on anything chasing us.

For the first time since getting the ten-minute call before the assault, I finally took my helmet off. Running my hand through my matted, sweaty hair, I forced all thoughts of jets and air-to-air missiles out of my head. We had roughly forty-five minutes until we got back to Jalalabad, and I didn't want to sit there and worry. I was grateful when Tom gave us something to do.

"Let's search the body again and make sure we didn't miss anything."

Walt climbed off of Bin Laden's chest and put on a pair of rubber gloves. I slid the zipper down, and we pulled the bag open, exposing the body. Walt started to pat him down, first in front, and then he slid his hands along the body's sides and back. Then we checked the pockets in his pants. We were looking for pocket litter—papers with phone numbers and other information.

As Walt searched, I noticed the crew chiefs on the helicopter were trying to get a look at the body. They'd scan outside the door and then steal a peek over their shoulder at the body. We waved them over and I shined a red-lens flashlight on Bin Laden's face.

Their eyes lit up. They kept smiling. I could see both felt proud to be part of the mission. We had trained with them since the first days in North Carolina. Without these guys, there was no mission. They safely negotiated the Pakistani air defenses and now were minutes from getting us home. Seeing their excitement, I got my first sense that this was going to be bigger than we'd imagined.

Walt didn't find anything. He zipped the bag up and returned to his seat on Bin Laden's chest.

I closed my eyes and started to process what happened. Just more than an hour ago, I thought we were all going to die in a helicopter crash. It was funny, the crash stuck with me a lot longer than getting shot at through the door. I'd been in firefights, but the crash was a first. It happened in slow motion. I had time to think about it. I could feel tightness in my chest creeping in as I thought about falling out of the sky. I could see the ground rushing up at us.

I had no control, and that scared me the most.

Part of me felt like we had failed despite the body at my feet. We weren't able to get as much intelligence as we could have. We left drawers unopened. The hallway on the second deck had stacks of boxes untouched. We usually did a better job, but we just ran out of time. We were perfectionists, and while the rest of the operation went smoothly after the crash, the SSE wasn't up to standards.

We were always our own worst critics.

The radio squawked in my ear, shaking me from my daze.

"We're back in Afghan airspace," Tom said.

I'd find out later that we had a good head start, and the jets never got close to catching us.

Fifteen minutes later, I could see the ring of bright lights in Jalalabad. It was a scene I'd experienced hundreds of times, and this time didn't feel much different. I knew that we'd made it back and in a few minutes we'd be on the ground and safe.

The helicopter set down just outside of the hangar. The protective halo of lights was on, and a white Toyota Hilux pickup was waiting for us on the tarmac.

As we climbed out, I could see three Army Rangers from the truck coming up to get the body. They'd been tasked with taking it from J-bad to Bagram.

The soldiers were led by a first sergeant who I'd worked with on my last rotation. He was still in the country since I'd gone home a month earlier. We'd run into each other a few times in the chow hall before the mission. He was squared away. We had a relationship of mutual respect.

But as they started to come toward the cabin to grab the body, we waved them off. This was our mission.

"Fuck no," Walt barked. "We got this."

We'd gone all the way to Pakistan to get him. We needed to see this thing all the way through.

I grabbed a handle on the body bag and we carried it to the back of the truck. I jumped on the tailgate, sitting backward. I could see everybody else piling out of the CH-47 and for a second felt a huge weight being lifted off my shoulders. Everyone made it back safely.

As we drove, the first sergeant grabbed my shoulder. When I looked up, he had his hand out with a 75th Ranger Regiment coin in his palm.

"You'll be my son's hero for the rest of his life," the first sergeant said. "Congratulations."

I nodded. I was really just happy that everyone was alive and home safe. We didn't have time to think about legacy.

CHAPTER 18

Confirmation

Just inside the hangar, I saw Admiral McRaven.

He was standing by himself near the door with his hands in his pockets. He must have come over from the Joint Operations Center as soon as he heard the radio call that we crossed the border.

The truck stopped just outside the door of the hangar, and he came over to the back near the tailgate. He seemed eager to see the body.

"Let's see him," McRaven said.

"OK, sir," I said, sliding off the tailgate.

I grabbed the bottom of the body bag and pulled it off the truck. It flopped on the cement floor like a dead fish. Kneeling down, I unzipped the bag. Almost all of the color had faded from his face and his skin looked ashy and gray. The body was mushy, and congealed blood had pooled at the bottom of the bag.

"There's your boy," I said.

McRaven, dressed in his tan digital camouflage uniform, stood over Bin Laden as I grabbed his beard and pulled his head to each side so the admiral could see his profile.

"He obviously just dyed his beard," I said. "He doesn't look as old as I expected he would."

I stood up and backed away as the others gathered around the body. Many of the guys from the other helicopters hadn't seen him yet. Soon, there was a crowd around McRaven, who had knelt down to get a better look.

"He is supposed to be six foot four," McRaven said, scanning the crowd.

I saw him point.

"How tall are you?"

One of the SEALs answered. "Six four," he said.

"Do you mind lying down next to him?" McRaven said.

After a quick double take to make sure McRaven wasn't just fucking with him, the SEAL got down beside the body bag as McRaven eyeballed the measurement.

"OK. OK," McRaven said. "Stand back up."

The measurement was mostly a joke. But Bin Laden didn't look quite like we had imagined. I am sure McRaven was having the same thoughts I had back on the third deck.

Standing at the edge of the crowd, I saw Jen. She looked

pale and stressed under the bright lights of the hangar. Guys were still walking into the hangar when she saw Ali. He smiled at her and she started crying. A couple of the SEALs put their arms around her and walked her over to the edge of the group to look at the body, which surprised me.

A few days before in the chow hall, Jen had told me she didn't want to see Bin Laden's body.

"I have no interest in seeing it," she told me. "My job description doesn't include having to look at a dead body."

I was sure this was some sort of bravado. She didn't have to get dirty in her line of work. She wore expensive high heels and she didn't worry about carrying dead weight to a waiting helicopter. She'd beaten Bin Laden on an intellectual level.

"If we pull this off," I had told her from across the table, "you've got to see the body."

Back in the hangar, Jen stayed on the perimeter of the crowd. She didn't say anything, but I knew from her reaction she could see Bin Laden's body on the floor. With tears rolling down her cheeks, I could tell it was taking a while for Jen to process. She'd spent half a decade tracking this man. And now there he was at her feet.

It was easier for us.

We saw dead bodies all the time. It was the kind of ugly we lived with, and we spent no time thinking about once it was finished. We were not jaded warmongers, but if you've seen one dead body, you've seen them all.

People at Jen's level never had to deal with the blood. So

to finally see Bin Laden's body at her feet must have been jarring.

I wandered away from the crowd. Leaning against the truck, I set down my rifle on the tailgate and stuffed my gloves into one of my cargo pockets. Most of the guys were back now and coming into the hangar. There were a lot of smiles.

Teddy was one of the last guys to walk into the hangar. I could tell by his face he was mad and maybe even a little embarrassed by the helicopter crash. I intercepted him as he walked into the hangar and gave him a crushing bear hug.

"Teddy," I said. "You're the heat."

He gave me a sheepish smile and tried to wiggle out of my grip.

"Dude, seriously," I said.

I know for a fact he kept the mission on track by ditching the way he did. Everybody was focused on who pulled the trigger but it was a lot harder to land a crashing helicopter than it was for any of us to pull the trigger. One wrong move and we all would have been in a pile of debris in the courtyard. Teddy saved all of our lives.

"Strong work," Walt said, giving me a handshake that turned into a hug.

For the next few minutes, we all rotated around, congratulating one another. People were still coming into the hangar. I don't remember who I talked to as much as I do how it felt to be back safe.

It didn't take long for the shit-talking to start.

"Blow up the house? Really?" I heard Charlie say to the EOD guy.

Eventually, we got together for a few posed pictures. We were one big team. As soon as the picture-taking ended, we all went back into work mode. Our five minutes of fun was over and it was time to get to Bagram to get the intelligence processed.

The Rangers had already packed up the body and were on their way to Bagram. We were following close behind in another plane. On the flight line, we loaded all our gear and strapped it down to the deck of the C-130. We walked on board still wearing our kit and carrying our weapons. There were few seats, so I found a spot near the front of the plane and sat down.

Nearby, I could see Jen sobbing. She was sitting on the floor, hugging her legs to her chest in the fetal position. I could just make out her eyes in the red light of the cabin. They were puffy, and she seemed to be staring into the distance. I got up and tapped her on the shoulder.

"Hey, it was one hundred percent!" I said, leaning close so she could hear over the roar of the engines.

She looked at me in a daze.

"Seriously, no shit," I said. "It was one hundred percent."

She nodded this time and started crying again. I scrambled back to my seat on the floor as the aircrew shut the cabin lights off. Minutes later, we were airborne and headed to Bagram. For most of the forty-five-minute flight I zoned out. I didn't really sleep but just rested. I knew we had hours of work left to do.

The C-130 let us out at a hangar along the flight line. Inside, a small cadre of FBI and CIA specialists waited to help us go through all the papers, thumb drives, and computers we recovered from the compound. As we walked into the hangar, it caught me off guard to see that the analysts were all standing at their individual tables with their hands folded behind them like in military parade rest.

A ring of tables with green plastic tubs full of food sat in one corner. Piled high in the containers were chicken fingers and French fries. A large coffee maker was pumping out one awful cup of coffee after another. It had been at least seven hours since we had eaten breakfast, but nobody touched the food. We had work to do.

Just inside the door, we started to offload our gear. As I pulled off my kit, I could feel pain shoot through my shoulder. It wasn't sharp, but there was a nagging, dull ache. I tried to push my shoulder forward enough to get a look, but I couldn't see any blood.

"Hey, Walt, is there something on my shoulder?" I asked.

He was unloading his gear too.

"It doesn't look like anything crazy," he said. "Looks like you caught some frag. Not bad enough where you need to get stitches."

Inspecting my gear, I grabbed the bolt cutters on my back

and felt a shard of metal cut into my fingertip. Holding the bolt cutters in my hand, I saw a good-size chunk of shrapnel embedded in the handle.

"From a bullet," I thought.

When al-Kuwaiti opened fire, fragments from the rounds must have hit me before I fired back. The cutters rode high on my back, so the handle was only a few inches from my head. I was damn lucky none of the shrapnel hit me in the neck.

After a quick after-action review to go over the mission, we started to unload all of the stuff we'd taken from the house. It had been ingrained in us from BUD/S to take care of team gear, then department gear, and then personal gear.

We divided the tables into groups corresponding with each room on the target. I took all of my bags to the table for the main compound, third deck, room A. Opening the mesh sack, I started to unload the stuff I collected. I stacked the tapes I'd taken off his dresser and put the pistol and rifle on the table.

On the white board, we drew a diagram of the inside of the compound and then laid out floor plans for the main building and the guesthouse. I took my camera over to where one of the SEALs was helping the CIA analyst download all the pictures from our digital cameras.

"How are all the pics coming out so far?" I asked, handing over my camera.

"So far so good," he said.

As the images of Bin Laden's body popped up on his screen, I was relieved. Since we had the body, the pictures weren't absolutely vital anymore. But I could just imagine if I fucked up the pictures I would never hear the end it from Charlie and Walt.

"You good?" I asked.

"Looks good here," the analyst said. "That's all we need."

I had no idea if the photos would ever be made public, and frankly I didn't care. That decision was well above my level and out of my control. I could hear the guys talking to the CIA analysts about the stuff they'd gathered.

"Dude, we're so sorry," said one of my teammates who searched the second deck. "There was so much more stuff. We didn't have enough time. We could have done better."

The CIA analyst almost laughed when he heard my teammate.

"You're good," he said. "Stop worrying about it. Look at all this shit. This is going to take us months to go through it all. We got more here than we've gotten in the past ten years."

The intelligence turnover took more than two hours. At the front of the hangar and about thirty feet away from the tables, I could see the FBI's DNA specialist taking samples from Bin Laden's body. As soon as he was finished, the Rangers escorted the body to the USS *Carl Vinson* for burial.

Finished with the SSE turnover, I started packing up my op gear. I cleared and safed my weapon, switched off the optics, and packed it in its case. Hoisting my kit onto the table, I stripped off the unused grenade and explosive charge. There was no reason to bring them home.

I was just finishing up when Jen and Ali came over. They

were leaving in a few minutes to fly back to the United States. The Air Force had an empty C-17 waiting to take them home.

She gave me a hug.

"I don't know when we'll see you guys again," she said, walking toward the door with Ali. "Be safe."

She had months of intelligence to sift through based on the raid, which would keep her busy. But unlike us, this hunt had been her life. Walking away, she seemed relieved and exhausted at the same time. For someone who spent most of the last decade trying to find him, I'm sure it wasn't something she could easily walk away from.

With most of our gear packed up, guys started snacking on some of the cold food. We made our way over to the large-screen TV that had been set up at the back of the hangar. President Obama was about to speak. Everybody stopped and huddled around it.

Rumor had it that JSOC had reviewed the speech to make sure the details of the mission were kept secret. Nobody doubted that details would eventually leak but at this point, I think we all just hoped that President Obama could keep a secret for a little while.

"I give it a week before they say SEALs were involved," I said to Walt.

"Shit, I don't even give it a day," he said.

At around 9:45 P.M. Eastern Time, the White House announced Obama was going to address the nation. By 10:30, the first leaks about Bin Laden were making the rounds. Navy Reserve intelligence officer Keith Urbahn was credited with breaking the news on Twitter. Soon, all of the major newspapers and TV news stations were reporting that Bin Laden was dead.

At 11:35 P.M., President Obama appeared on television. He walked down a long hall and took his position behind the podium. Staring straight into the camera, he told the world what we had done.

"Good evening. Tonight, I can report to the American people and to the world that the United States has conducted an operation that killed Osama bin Laden, the leader of al Qaeda, and a terrorist who's responsible for the murder of thousands of innocent men, women, and children."

We all listened quietly.

Obama went on to thank the military for hunting al Qaeda and protecting American citizens.

"We've disrupted terrorist attacks and strengthened our homeland defense. In Afghanistan, we removed the Taliban government, which had given Bin Laden and al Qaeda safe haven and support. And around the globe, we worked with our friends and allies to capture or kill scores of al Qaeda terrorists, including several who were a part of the 9/11 plot," Obama said.

The president stressed that soon after being elected, he told Leon Panetta to make killing or capturing Bin Laden a priority and outlined how we found him. That part of the speech was deftly crafted and didn't reveal any harmful details.

"Today, at my direction, the United States launched a targeted operation against that compound in Abbottabad, Pakistan. A small team of Americans carried out the operation with extraordinary courage and capability," Obama said. "No Americans were harmed. They took care to avoid civilian casualties. After a firefight, they killed Osama bin Laden and took custody of his body."

None of us were huge fans of Obama. We respected him as the commander in chief of the military and for giving us the green light on the mission.

"You know we just put admiral's stars on Jay," Walt said during the speech. "And we just got this guy reelected."

"Well, would you rather not have done this?" I said.

We all knew the deal.

We were tools in their toolbox, and when things go well they promote it. They inflate their roles. But we should have done it. It was the right call to make. Regardless of the politics that would come along with it, the end result was what we all wanted.

"McRaven will be running SOCOM in a year and will probably be CNO someday," I said.

Obama called the mission the "most significant achievement to date in our nation's effort to defeat al Qaeda" and thanked us for our sacrifice.

"The American people do not see their work, nor know their names," he said.

We'd expected him to give away details. If he had, we could have talked some smack. But I didn't think his speech was bad at all. If anything, it was kind of anticlimactic.

"OK, enough of this," I said to Walt. "Let's go find some food or at least a hot shower."

Word went out we had a flight home in a few hours. I found my backpack with my civilian clothes and boarded a bus for the JSOC compound. The team decided to try and squeeze in showers before heading back to Virginia Beach.

The compound had a handful of shower trailers. Standing under the scalding water, I could feel my body slowly starting to unwind.

Plus, I was hungry.

DEVGRU has a small section of the JSOC compound. It was our ground mobility shop. Basically, they kept all of our trucks, motorcycles, four-wheelers, and Humvees working. A SEAL headed it up and worked with a bunch of Seabees and mechanics.

The flight home got delayed a few hours, so we made ourselves at home. Inside the work area, the garage was littered with parts, tools, and vehicles in all phases of repair. We gathered in a small office area with a sitting room and lounge. The SEAL who ran the shop welcomed us with open arms.

"What do you need?" he said.

Comprised of a few modular buildings and a covered motor pool, they had carved out a small patio with a brick pizza oven and a large gas grill. Walt walked around the patio passing around a box of cigars the NRA had sent him weeks before to welcome him home from deployment. They had no idea we'd smoke them to celebrate the mission that killed Bin Laden.

Everybody was there except Jay, Mike, and Tom. The head shed were still over at the airfield briefing Admiral McRaven.

We spent most of the time on the patio soaking up the warm spring sun. The Seabees who lived at the compound were firing up the grill to cook steaks and lobster tail they had liberated from the chow hall. I could smell popcorn in the office and pizza cooking in the brick oven.

I was half asleep on the patio getting some sun when I heard someone yell out.

"You guys aren't going to believe this shit. It's already out."

At one of the computer terminals, the team leader of the perimeter security team was reading the news sites. It took less than four hours before the news was reporting that it was SEALs who had carried out the mission. Then it was SEALs from DEVGRU based in Virginia Beach.

The mission had been secret for almost a month now, and suddenly it was all over the news. We watched footage of the crowds that spontaneously gathered outside the White House, Ground Zero, and the Pentagon. At a Major League baseball game in Philadelphia, fans started to chant "U-S-A." Everyone commented about how young they looked. Kids like that didn't know what the United States was like before September 11, 2001.

We watched the madness on TV, and I couldn't help but wonder what my friends and family were thinking back at home. Nobody knew I was in Afghanistan. I told my parents I was out of town training and wouldn't have my cell phone. I was sure everybody was calling my phone trying to see where I was.

The sun was warm as we sat outside and ate. Now full, all I could think about was sleep. The bus came back a few hours later to take us to the plane. The adrenaline was gone as we dragged ourselves on board.

The C-17 was empty except for the aircrew.

Our containers boarded first and then we followed, spreading our ground pads on the deck. As we got settled, I could see the crew chiefs talking with the pilots. Air Force C-17 flights are always hit or miss. Sometimes you'll score a cool aircrew that will let you sleep wherever you want, while others are by-the-book and keep you in your seats.

As the plane's engines warmed up, the crew chief got on the intercom.

"Hey, guys, we're not stopping in Germany so we'll be getting gas from an airborne tanker in route back to the United States," he said. "You guys get some sleep."

They obviously figured out who their passengers were, and the crew was cool enough to let us get some much-needed sleep. Typically, we stop in Germany for gas. Everybody was stoked the aircrew was going to be cool and that we were going to fly straight through. At this point we'd been up for almost twenty-four hours. Takeoff was quiet and then the plane headed west.

We were spent.

The media blitz we had just seen on TV and online was jarring. I don't think anybody was prepared for it. But stretching out on the deck of the C-17, I didn't have the energy to give a shit. My mind needed to turn off.

I took two Ambien and was fast asleep before we got out of Afghan airspace.

CHAPTER 19

Touch the Magic

My phone vibrated, pinged, buzzed, and beeped as it started to receive a day's worth of messages.

Seconds after our C-17 landed in Virginia Beach, every one of us turned on a phone to a cacophony of ring tones. I placed my phone next to me while it practically popped like corn in a kettle.

While we cruised over the Atlantic, news of the raid dominated TV and the Web. Reporters flooded Virginia Beach searching for real live Navy SEALs to interview. In Washington, anyone on Capitol Hill or in the Pentagon who had even a shred of information was leaking it.

When my phone finally stopped, I started to scroll through

the messages. People had no idea I'd been on the raid. But anybody and everybody that knew I was a SEAL contacted me to talk about it. I had messages from my family and even friends from college who I hadn't talked to in years. All the messages were the same:

"Hey, buddy, what's going on? I'm watching the news. Just wondering if you're in town."

It was so top secret when we left that we weren't even telling people in our own unit where we were going. But now, I had close to one hundred e-mails, fifty voice mails, and three dozen text messages asking me if I happened to be in Pakistan or if I knew what was going on. My family just wanted to know if I was in town and safe.

The plane barely came to a stop when the crew door popped open and the old commander of our squadron sprinted aboard. He was waiting to take command of DEVGRU. They had delayed the change of command until after this mission, so he was not with us in Afghanistan. He was one of the best leaders I've ever worked for. All of the guys loved him because he always had our back.

As we gathered up our backpacks, he walked down the line giving everyone a handshake and hug. He wanted to be the first to welcome us back. We were still shaking off the haze of the Ambien, so it was kind of surreal to see his lanky frame and bald head move down the line. This was the first sign that our welcome home would be bigger than we anticipated.

The whine of the engines made it hard to hear as we got off the plane. It was pitch-black outside. Moving from the bright cabin into the night made it worse. It took a few seconds for my eyes to adjust, but when they did I saw about two hundred of my teammates lined up to greet us. I could make out their silhouettes as I walked toward the white buses that would take us to our base. It was about a fifty yard walk to the bus and I shook at least a hundred hands.

We always tried to meet the plane when squadrons returned home. It struck me that anybody standing in that line shaking our hands could have been in our shoes. We just happened to be at the right place at the right time. I felt really lucky.

I didn't have but a few seconds to yell out a hello or mumble a thank-you as I passed. We were exhausted and a little overwhelmed when we got to the bus.

Thankfully, there was a cooler full of beer and some hot pizza waiting for us. I settled silently into my seat. Holding my backpack between my legs, I balanced my phone on my thigh as I ate and sipped a beer. I looked around the bus. Everybody had their noses stuck in their phones trying to sift through the glut of messages. Roughly twenty-four hours ago, President Obama had addressed the nation about the raid.

For the first time, it started to sink in. This was pretty cool. It was the kind of mission I'd read about in Alaska as a kid. It was history. But just as quickly as those thoughts crossed my mind, I forced them out. The second you stop and believe your own hype, you've lost.

Back at the command, I didn't even go inside. Our gear and weapons were placed in our storage bay and locked. There was no need to unload everything, and we were lucky enough to have the next few days off work. I threw my civilian backpack into my truck and headed home. I didn't want to go out and hit the bars and celebrate. I just wanted some quiet. The welcome was overwhelming enough.

On the way home, I spotted the neon drive-through sign at the Taco Bell. I always stopped for a south of the border fix on my way home from a deployment, usually in Germany. I had made this stop several times over the years. Pulling into the line, I ordered two crispy tacos, a bean burrito, and a medium Pepsi.

At the window, a high school kid handed me my food and drink. I pulled forward into the parking lot and took out a taco. I spread the paper in my lap and drizzled some fire sauce over the cold, crisp lettuce and ate.

On the radio, I had the country music station playing. Between bites, I tried to make sense of everything. Days before, I'd been choking down chow hall food and trying to keep the mission out of my head. Now, I was eating Taco Bell in a parking lot on my way home and still trying to keep it out of my head.

I needed a few days off.

We joked before we left Bagram about getting some time off. I knew the rest of my squadron was off the coast of Virginia practicing underways. The command had rented a cruise ship and filled it with role players. It was a massive and expensive training event. It always sounded more fun than it really was. Inevitably, it turned into hours in the cold

284

water being pounded by waves as you climb up the side of a ship.

After the final bite of the bean burrito, I rolled up the paper and threw it back in the bag. Taking a big sip of my drink, I put my truck in gear and headed home. Before I could relax, I unpacked and took a long shower.

But I was still pretty wired. I had just slept for nineteen hours. The TV was on, and I started to surf the cable news channels. Every show was airing something related to the mission. Most of it was speculation.

They reported that we were in a forty-minute firefight.

Then I saw that we'd taken fire while we were outside the gate.

Then, Bin Laden had a weapon and attempted to defend himself before we shot him.

And of course it was reported, in Bin Laden's last seconds, he had enough time to look into our eyes and see that it was Americans coming to get him.

The raid was being reported like a bad action movie. At first, it was funny because it was so wrong.

But then photos of the compound flashed across the screen. For weeks it had been top secret and now here it was all over the news. I saw wreckage of the helicopter. The charges destroyed the fuselage but there was still a section of the tail rotor that survived. When the explosives detonated, the tail section broke off and fell onto the ground on the outside of the wall.

The Reuters wire service even had pictures of the bodies

we left behind. On the screen, shots of the al-Kuwaiti brothers—including Abrar, who Will and I shot through the door of the guesthouse—flashed on the screen. A picture of where Bin Laden's body had been came on next. I could see the dried blood on the rug.

I struggled to wrap my mind around it.

To see these images on prime-time television was hard for me to deal with. The images broke through the tiny compartment in my brain that I'd placed this whole experience in. I had no barrier between home and work now. I've always been good at mentally blocking out the "work" I'd done overseas. When I was home, I was home. Seeing these images was like crossing the two streams and it made my head hurt.

I didn't sleep well that night. I'd squirreled away a couple of Ambien. There was no way I was going to sleep without them.

For the next two days, I dodged calls from friends and family. My phone wouldn't stop ringing. My family was asking me if I was involved. My parents knew I'd been gone, but they didn't know where.

Before I left, I had called them and said I was going to train and wouldn't have phone service. I always tried to keep things vague with them. I had sent my sisters a random text message before we left simply telling them that I loved them both. It wasn't a red flag at the time, but after the news broke, my sisters knew I must be up to something.

The day after we got home, I was taking my trash can to the curb when my neighbor from across the street walked over and gave me a huge hug. She knew I was a SEAL and noticed I had been gone for a few days.

"You never really know what your neighbors do for a living, do you?" she said as she smiled and walked back to her house.

It was the same for my teammates. One buddy barely got in the door before he was back changing diapers.

"So I get home and she hands me my kid right away," my buddy said when we got back to work. "We just shot UBL. Think I can sit down and drink a beer?"

Another spent the morning after he got home mowing his overgrown lawn. We might have been getting the celebrity treatment in the media, but at home we were just absent husbands.

When we finally came back to work officially two days later, Jay called us into a meeting in the same conference room where we first heard about the mission. There was concern at the command level about all the leaks revolving around the raid.

"It is imperative that we stay out of the media," Jay said. "Let's all make sure we're keeping a low profile."

I was astonished. We'd kept this whole thing under wraps for weeks. Now, Washington was leaking everything, and we were going to get the lecture for it. It felt like it was only a matter of time before some of our names appeared on the news.

We just killed the number one terrorist in the world. The last thing we needed was our names attached to it. We simply wanted to fade back into the shadows and go back to work.

"With that out of the way," Jay said, "here is your schedule. Take a week off."

"But not a real week off, right," Walt said.

I heard a chuckle from some of the others.

"When does the dog and pony show start?" I said.

"The agency will be down in a few days," Jay said. "SecDef is also planning a visit soon. We will pass the word on the schedule once we have it. Enjoy the break."

This time I laughed.

"Come on, everybody wants to touch the magic," Tom said as we walked out of the conference room.

The mission hadn't been that complicated or difficult.

Weeks and months after the mission, details about the raid were appearing with a renewed focus on the unit. It raised a lot of concerns for our personal safety. Most of us had already invested in home security systems.

Some of us voiced concerns to Jay and Mike at what seemed like a weekly meeting.

"What if our names are leaked to the media?" I said.

ABC News had come out with a ridiculous story about how to spot a SEAL. Reporter Chris Cuomo reported that the SEAL who shot Bin Laden was probably a physically fit white man in his thirties with a beard and longer hair. Then Cuomo did what the other reporters did. They found any SEAL who would talk about us, in this case DEVGRU founder Richard Marcinko.

"They have gazelle legs, no waist, and a huge upper body configuration, and almost a mental block that says, 'I will not fail,'" Marcinko told Cuomo.

Other telltale traits: calloused hands from firing a weapon, shrapnel wounds from previous missions, and big egos.

"They are basically individual egomaniacs that make music together. They learn to depend on each other. When they are bored they play with each other to keep pushing. Otherwise, they get in trouble," Marcinko told ABC News.

We laughed our asses off. I know he was a founder of DEVGRU, but he was hopelessly out of touch with the modern force. I didn't know a single SEAL who fit his profile. We'd evolved past being egomaniacs. There wasn't a soldier, sailor, airman, or Marine in the special operations community that fit his profile. It wasn't part of our ethos. We were team players who always tried to do the right thing.

But we weren't in the meeting to talk about leaks and security concerns.

"Keep this on the down low because nobody knows this," Jay said. "You're going to meet the president in Kentucky tomorrow."

With the dog and pony circuit in full effect, we had assumed it was coming.

"We'll fly up in civilian clothes and then change into our uniforms to meet the president," Jay said.

They dismissed us, and we were done for the day. On the way to my truck, my phone buzzed.

It was a text message from my sister.

"I hear you're going to meet the president tomorrow," she said. "Make sure you don't wear shorts so they don't see your gazelle-type legs and know you're a SEAL."

So much for operational security.

The next morning, we left on one of the oldest C-130s I'd ever seen. It had a new paint job, which masked its age from the outside. But getting on board, the inside looked old. Everything was faded.

As we climbed up the ramp, none of us were impressed. We were used to flying around in much newer C-130s or even C-17s.

"So much for rock star status," Charlie said as he folded his six-foot-four frame into the orange jump seat. "I guess our fifteen minutes of fame are over."

But a plaque near the door told us the true story. The plane was one of three MC-130E Combat Talon I aircraft used in Operation Eagle Claw.

It turns out a crew chief found the plane mothballed and talked an Air Force general into renovating it and returning it to the inventory. It was sort of fitting that we'd fly to Kentucky to meet the president on that plane. It had a lot of history and I guess it had at least one more historic flight in it.

From the airport, we took back roads to the 160th Special Operations Aviation Regiment's headquarters, where Teddy and the aircrews were based. President Obama was scheduled to talk with thousands of troops from the 101st Airborne Division after meeting with us.

They ushered us into a large conference room to wait.

Along the back wall was a table piled high with gourmet sandwiches, chips, cookies, and soft drinks.

"We're moving up in the world," I said. "This is way better than cold chicken fingers. Do you think they are going to make us pay for this?"

On one of the tables near the door was a framed flag. It was one of the flags we carried on the mission. Guys were signing the back of the frame and the plan was to present it to the president.

"Why do I need to sign this?" I asked Tom.

Like always, he was running things while Jay and Mike met with the higher-ups.

"Everybody that was on the raid needs to sign it," he said.

"Why?" I just wanted an explanation.

"It's going to the president," Tom said, growing tired of my questions.

"How many hands does it pass through before it gets hung on the wall?" I asked. "Don't they have tours of the White House?"

The only thing that remained secret was our names.

I went over to the other guys.

"Is everybody signing this thing?"

Most of the guys had already signed it.

"Just scribble a random name on there and you'll be good," Charlie said. "That's what I did."

After a lot of hurry up and wait, we finally walked to an auditorium to meet the president. The Secret Service ran us through a metal detector. When they got to me, the wand beeped when it passed over my pocketknife. I took my knife out and added it to the growing pile.

There was a small stage with rows of chairs in front.

Walt sat down next to me.

"I'd rather be doing underways than be here," he said.

Obama arrived in a dark suit, white shirt, and light blue tie. Vice President Biden was at his side in a blue shirt and red tie. The president stood on the stage and spoke to us for a few minutes. He presented the unit with a Presidential Unit Citation, in recognition of our achievement. It is the highest honor that can be given to a unit.

I don't recall much about the speech. It was straight from the speechwriter playbook:

"You guys are America's best."

"You are what America stands for."

"Thank you from the American people."

"Job well done."

After the speech, we posed for a few pictures. Biden kept cracking lame jokes that no one got. He seemed like a nice guy, but he reminded me of someone's drunken uncle at Christmas dinner. Before leaving to give a speech to two thousand soldiers from the 101st, Obama invited the whole team to his residence for a beer.

"What is the residence?" I asked.

"I don't know," Walt said. "His house. The White House, I guess."

"That would be kind of cool," I said. "I wouldn't mind going to the residence."

Walt just smirked.

As the bus drove us to the airport, Obama delivered a speech to cheering soldiers in a hangar on the base.

"We have cut off their head," he said, "and we will ultimately defeat them . . . our strategy is working, and there is no greater evidence of that than justice finally being delivered to Osama bin Laden."

After that trip, things started to return to normal. We jumped back into our normal schedule, gone for a few weeks and then home for a week. We were back on the speeding train.

We never got the call to have a beer at the White House. I remember I brought it up a few months later to Walt. We'd just come back from the range and we were walking back into the team room.

"Hey, did you ever hear anything about that beer?" I asked.

Walt's smirk was back.

"You believed that shit," he said. "I bet you voted for change too, sucker."

Epilogue

Less than a year after the Bin Laden mission, I got off the speeding train.

I'd spent over a decade of my life sacrificing for this job and country. I gave up everything to live this dream. Long periods spent away from friends and family, missed holidays, and a physical beating on my body that will last the rest of my life. I served with America's best and made lifelong friends with a group of guys I call my brothers. Since my first deployment as a SEAL and the attacks on September 11, I'd dreamt of being involved in the mission that would kill or capture Osama bin Laden. I was lucky enough to play a role. Now, it is time for someone else to take a turn.

Very few people can say that they were lucky enough to stay in an operational job their entire SEAL career. From the day I graduated BUD/S, I moved to SEAL Team Five and then on to DEVGRU. I never worked a nonoperational job. In more than a decade as a SEAL, I didn't have a break, just a steady drumbeat of combat deployments. After finishing my team leader time earlier this year, I was slated to leave my squadron and either be an instructor in Green Team or work one of several other nonoperational jobs within the command. These jobs were far from the battlefield and, to be perfectly honest, probably just the break that I needed. I knew after that short break, I would be itching to get back into the fight. Like everyone at the command, my personal life suffered under the strain of deployments. It was time for my own life to take a priority. As much as I hated leaving the command, it was time for me to move on and end my career as a SEAL.

Before I left, I met with the commander who welcomed us home after the raid. He was now the acting commander of DEVGRU. I knew that as a well-respected commanding officer, he actually understood the stresses we lived under. We met in his office a few days before I was scheduled to sign out of the command.

"What can we do to keep you?" the commander said.

I was honored he wanted me to stay. But I looked him in the eye and humbly shook my head.

"It's time for me to move on," I said.

Although I felt a certain amount of guilt, like I was leaving my brothers behind to carry the load, I was at peace with my decision. There were newer guys, fresh from Green Team, who were primed and ready to lead the fight. I was simply tired and ready for something new.

It was strange to leave Walt, Charlie, Steve, and Tom behind. We are all still friends, and all four are still at the command. For their protection, I'm not going to talk much about what the guys are doing now. They are all still sacrificing their lives and time for the good of this country.

Phil fully recovered from the gunshot wound in his calf. He is still a tier-one prankster and remains one of my best friends. Like me, he is no longer in the Navy, having retired after his injury.

One of my first projects after leaving was this book. Deciding to do it wasn't easy. No one at the command thought much of the notoriety that came after the Bin Laden raid. We watched it with amusement at first, but that quickly turned to dread as more and more information leaked. We always prided ourselves for being the quiet professionals, but the more I saw coverage of the raid, the more I wanted to set the record straight.

To date, how the mission to kill Bin Laden has been reported is wrong. Even reports claiming to have the inside story have been incorrect. I felt like someone had to tell the true story. To me, the story is bigger than the raid itself and much more about the men at the command who willingly go into harm's way, sacrificing all they have to do the job. Theirs is a story that deserves to be told, and told as accurately as possible.

Since May 1, 2011, everyone from President Obama to

Admiral McRaven has given interviews about the operation. If my commander in chief is willing to talk, then I feel comfortable doing the same.

Of course, the raid is now being used in a political wrestling match as both parties fight for the White House. The mission was never about that for the twenty-four men who climbed on board the helicopters that night. Politics are for the Washington, D.C., policy makers who safely watched the action on a video monitor from thousands of miles away.

When we boarded our helicopters in Jalalabad, politics was the last thing on our minds. Don't get me wrong. We weren't oblivious to it. We knew this was going to happen. Does it play a role in the aftermath? Of course it does, but I don't think it matters if a Republican or a Democrat gave the order. It doesn't make me vote for one party more than another.

Let me be clear, I do not consider this to be my story. My goal from the start was to tell the true story of the raid and show the sacrifices made by SEALs at the command. I only used my life as a way to describe what it is like to be part of such a special unit. I am not unique or special, and my hope is my experiences are viewed as a common experience for all of the men I served with. The men I looked up to, the men I worked with, those men are the best in the world and have done more for this country than people will ever comprehend.

For the fallen SEALs who didn't make it home, their sacrifice is not in vain. Some were lost fighting in Iraq or Afghanistan. Others died training to fight. We hold all of them close to our hearts and know they died for something so much bigger then themselves. Despite knowing the risks, men like these continue to willingly sacrifice everything.

I challenge every person who reads this to sacrifice a little something as well. I've been asked a question: "I'm not a SEAL and probably couldn't do it if I tried, but what can I do to help?"

Two answers come to mind.

Don't just live, but live for a purpose bigger than yourself. Be an asset to your family, community, and country.

The second answer is that you can donate time and money to a veterans' organization or one that supports wounded warriors. These men and women have done their part and need our help.

I'm donating the majority of the proceeds from this book to charity. Here are several that I recommend.

> All In All The Time Foundation
> (Allinallthetime.org)
>
> The Navy SEAL Foundation
> (Navysealfoundation.org)
>
> Tip of the Spear Foundation
> (Tipofthespearfoundation.org)

All three charities help support the families of fallen Navy SEALs. I challenge you to do a fraction of what these men have sacrificed and help me raise millions of dollars for these organizations.

I am telling this story and donating most of the proceeds from its sale in honor of the men we have lost since September 11. They are the true heroes.

THOMAS C. FOUKE
Lieutenant

THOMAS RATZLAFF
SOCS

STEPHEN MILLS
SOC

ROBERT REEVES
SOCS

NICHOLAS SPEHAR
SO2

NICHOLAS NULL
EODC

MICHAEL STRANGE
CTR1

MATTHEW MASON
SOC

LOUIS LANGLAIS
SOCM

KRAIG VICKERS
EODCS

KEVIN HOUSTON
SOC

JONAS KELSALL
LCDR (SEAL)

JON TUMILSON
SO1

JOHN FAAS
SOC

JOHN DOUANGDARA
MA1

JESSE PITTMAN
SO1

JASON WORKMAN
SO1

JARED DAY
IT1

HEATH ROBINSON
SOCS

DARRIK BENSON
SO1

CHRISTOPHER CAMPBELL
SO1

CALEB A. NELSON
SO1

BRIAN BILL
SOC

AARON VAUGHN
SO1

TYLER STIMSON
SO1

RONALD WOODLE
SO2

DENIS CHRISTOPHER MIRANDA
SO3

DAVID BLAKE MCLENDON
CTRCS

COLLIN THOMAS
SOC

BRENDAN JOHN LOONEY
LT

ADAM OLIN SMITH
SO2

ADAM BROWN
SOC

TYLER J. TRAHAN
EOD2

RYAN JOB
SO2

ERIC F. SHELLENBERGER
SOC

ANDREW J. LIGHTNER
PR1

THOMAS J. VALENTINE
SOCS

SHAPOOR "ALEX" GHANE
SO2

NATHAN HARDY
SOC

MICHAEL KOCH
SOC

LUIS SOUFFRONT
EOD1

LANCE M. VACCARO
SOC

JOSHUA THOMAS HARRIS
SO1

JOHN W. MARCUM
SOCS

JASON R. FREIWALD
SOC (Select)

STEVEN P. DAUGHERTY
CTT1

ROBERT R. MCRILL
MC1

MARK T. CARTER
SOC

JOSEPH CLARK SCHWEDLER
SO2

JASON D. LEWIS
SO1

FREDDIE PORTER
SN

MICHAEL A. MONSOOR
MA2 (SEAL)

MARC A. LEE
AO2 (SEAL)

SHANE E. PATTON
MM2 (SEAL)

MICHAEL P. MURPHY
LT (SEAL)

MICHAEL M. MCGREEVY, JR.
LT (SEAL)

MATTHEW G. AXELSON
STG2 (SEAL)

JEFFREY S. TAYLOR
HM1 (SEAL)

JEFFREY A. LUCAS
ET1 (SEAL)

JAMES SUH
QM2 (SEAL)

JACQUES J. FONTAN
FCC (SEAL)

ERIK S. KRISTENSEN
LCDR (SEAL)

DANNY P. DIETZ
GM2 (SEAL)

DANIEL R. HEALY
ITCS (SEAL)

THEODORE D. FITZHENRY
HMCS (SEAL)

ROBERT P. VETTER
BM1 (SWCC)

BRIAN OUELLETTE
BM1 (SEAL)

THOMAS E. RETZER
IC1 (SEAL)

MARIO MAESTAS
IT2 (SEAL)

DAVID M. TAPPER
PH1 (SEAL)

PETER G. OSWALD
CDR (SEAL)

NEIL C. ROBERTS
ABH1 (SEAL)

MATTHEW J. BOURGEOIS
HMC (SEAL)

JERRY "BUCK" POPE
ENS (SEAL)

*List courtesy Navy SEAL Foundation

CONFIRMING SOURCES

Ackman, Dan. "The Cost of Being Osama Bin Laden."
Forbes Magazine, September 14, 2001.

Associated Press. "Jimmy Carter: Iran hostage rescue should
have worked." *USA Today*, September 17, 2010.

Bowden, Mark. *Black Hawk Down: A Story of Modern War.*
New York: Signet, 2002.

Butcher, Mike. "Here's the guy who unwittingly live-tweeted
the raid on Bin Laden." *TechCrunch*, May 2, 2011.

Chalker, Dennis, and Kevin Dockery. *One Perfect Op: Navy
SEAL Special Warfare Teams.* New York: Avon Books,
2002.

Eggen, Dan. "Bin Laden, Most Wanted For Embassy
Bombings?" *The Washington Post*, August 28, 2006.

Encyclopædia Britannica Online, 11th ed. "Abbottabad," http://en.wikisource.org/wiki/1911_ Encyclop%C3%A6dia_Britannica/Abbottabad.

FBI. "FBI Ten Most Wanted Fugitives." Archived from the original on January 3, 2008.

Fury, Dalton. *Kill Bin Laden*. New York: St. Martin's Press, 2008.

Goldman, Adam, and Matt Apuzzo. "Phone call by Kuwaiti courier led to bin Laden." *PilotOnline*, May 3, 2011.

Graham, Maureen, and Troy Graham. "Navy SEAL killed in Afghanistan was part of Lynch rescue." *Philadelphia Inquirer*. August 22, 2003.

Hagerman, Bart, ed. *USA Airborne: 50th Anniversary*. Paducah, KY: Turner Publishing Company, 1990.

Marcinko, Richard. *Rogue Warrior*. New York: Pocket Books, 1992.

Mayer, Jane. *The Dark Side: The Inside Story of How the War on Terror Turned Into a War on American Ideals*. New York: Random House, 2008.

Miller, Greg. "CIA flew stealth drones into Pakistan to monitor bin Laden house." *The Washington Post*, May 17, 2011.

"'Most wanted terrorists' list released." CNN.com, October 10, 2001.

Murdico, Suzanne J. *Osama Bin Laden*. Rosen Publishing Group, 2004.

Schmidle, Nicholas. "A Reporter At Large: Getting Bin Laden: What happened that night in Abbottabad." *The New Yorker*, August 8, 2011.

Smith, Michael. *Killer Elite: The Inside Story of America's Most Secret Special Operations Team*. New York: St. Martin's Press, 2007.

United States Army. 160th Special Operations Aviation Regiment. *160th SOAR(A) Green Platoon Train-up program*. Archived from the original on May 31, 2008.

Mark Owen is a former member of the United States Naval Special Warfare Development Group, commonly known as SEAL Team Six. In his many years as a Navy SEAL, he has participated in hundreds of missions around the globe, including the rescue of Captain Richard Phillips in the Indian Ocean in 2009. Owen was a team leader on Operation Neptune Spear in Abbottabad, Pakistan, on May 1, 2011, which resulted in the death of Osama bin Laden. Owen was one of the first men through the door on the third floor of the terrorist mastermind's hideout, where he witnessed Bin Laden's death. Mark Owen's name and the names of the other SEALs mentioned in *No Easy Day* have been changed for their security.

Kevin Maurer has covered special operations forces for nine years. He has been embedded with the Special Forces in Afghanistan six times, spent a month in 2006 with special operations units in east Africa, and has embedded with U.S. forces in Iraq and Haiti. He is the author of four books, including several about special operations.